Voice of the Ancestors V.III

Guns & Butter

Chase McGhee

Chase McGhee

Voice of the Ancestors Volume III

Copyright © 2021 by Chase McGhee

Published in the United States of America

DEDICATION

This book is dedicated to the late great Ermias Asghedom otherwise known as Nipsey Hussle. May your courageous spirit continue to lead and guide us to true freedom and liberation.

Long Live Nip

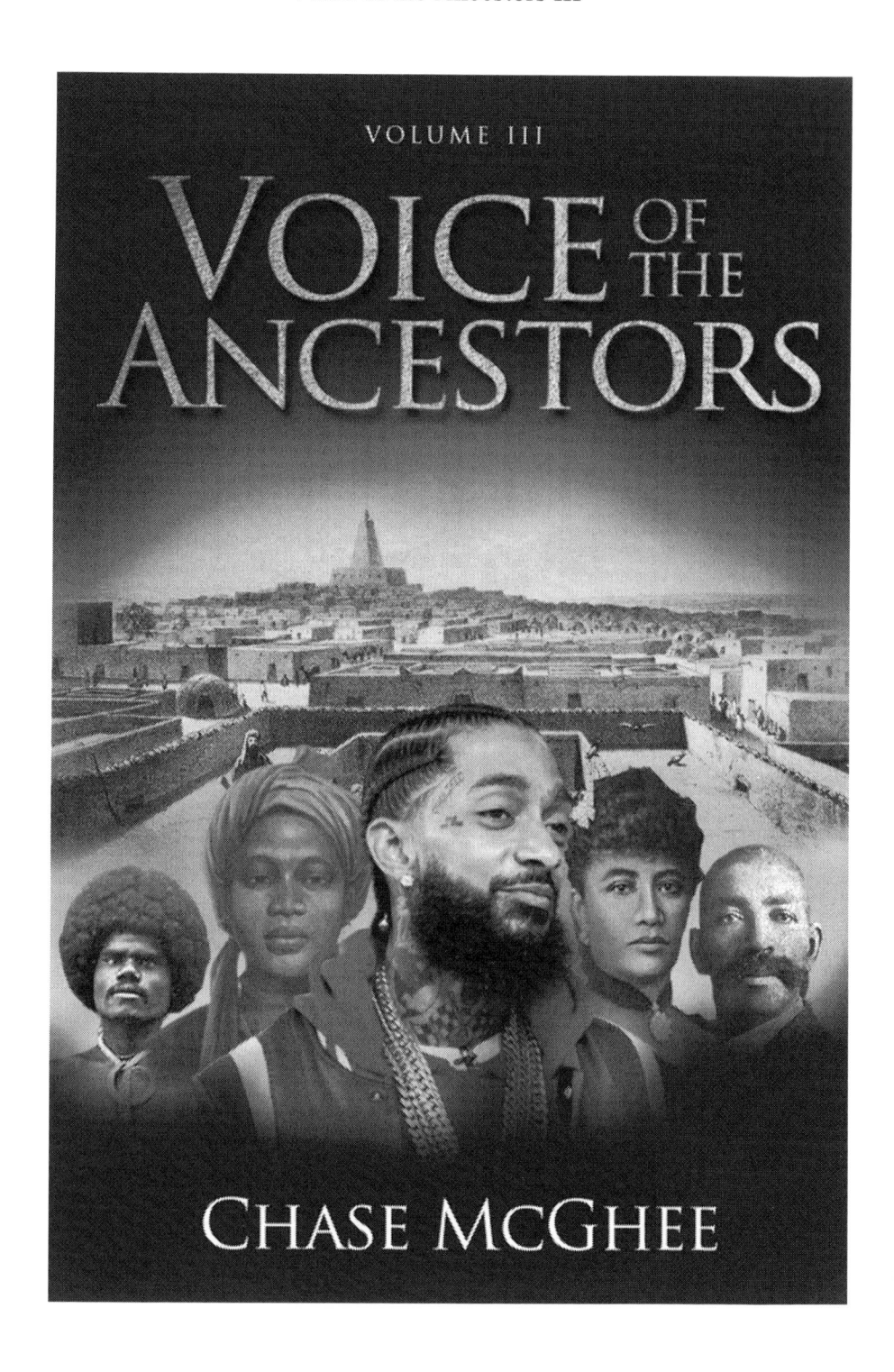

Chase McGhee

ACKNOWLEDGMENTS

Special thanks and acknowledgement to these special individuals for their constant love and support throughout this long process. For without you the creation of this book would not have been possible.

- **Alegna Kween, London, U.K. (Editor)**
- **April Brown, United States (Editor)**
- Colleen McGhee, Atlanta, Georgia
- Chanlor McGhee, Atlanta, Georgia
- Raymond McGhee, Atlanta, Georgia
- Connie Raines, Conyers, Georgia
- Joshua Patrick, Atlanta, Georgia
- Kyle Bailey, Atlanta, Georgia
- Precious Mmegwa, Nigeria
- Joel Mccandless, Birmingham, Alabama
- Chelsi Bender, New Jersey
- Milton Duggin Jr., Tuscaloosa, Alabama
- Cliff Avril, Seattle, Washington
- Stephen Collins, Denver, Colorado

Introduction

Finally, the time has come for the last and final installment of the Voice of the Ancestors Series, *Volume III: Guns and Butter*. In volume I and II of the series we primarily talked about the importance of breaking out the shackles and chains of mental enslavement by regaining knowledge of self and never forgiving or forgetting who and how those chains were put on. Well in Volume III, we will break down the Guns and butter of the game. The guns being the assets we will need to make for a more sturdy and strong foundation. These Guns will come in the form of not only physical weapons but financial ones, that will be used to build and protect our new thriving communities. Yet, along with guns we will also add a little butter, a substance that is rich and used to enhance the flavor of things. Our butter is our history, something that is rich in substance and when understood properly in our case can be used to enhance our guns. As stated, before in previous volumes, one can easily obtained knowledge of defense and economics but if they do not understand history, they will lose it all. Which is why in this book we will connect all three, knowledge of self, Economics, and Military science. In order to make sure we regain what's rightfully ours, by any means necessary!

Part. 1

Black Magic

"Sometimes as Black People, we have to look ourselves in the mirror, and remind ourselves we have the juice".

-Chase McGhee

There is an old saying that sometimes you have to laugh to keep from crying. A saying I feel all black people in America and around the world can relate to. When we look at our history of mistreatment from all races including ourselves, it's easy to feel sad and helpless. It becomes easy to accept the false narratives that we as black people are not smart or civilized human beings. In the past some would use the Old Scofield Reference Bible to justify their racist behavior.
 Saying that African people were the children of Canaan who would be born ugly, black, and only fit to be slaves. A stereotype that would be instilled onto us by the

dominant society. However, as we proved in "Voice of the Ancestors" Volume I and II and will continue to prove throughout this book, we are far from the racist stereotypes instilled upon us. Which is why to kick this book off we are going to take a more detailed look at our accomplishments, discoveries, and inventions.

While also focusing on our natural god given abilities as black people and how we have used those abilities to empower ourselves as well as others. This whole book in a sense, is a testament to the black magic and capabilities that lives within all our people. Therefore, I want you to sit back, take notes and enjoy to visualize and harness the black magic within.

The Black Presence around the World

Members of the dominant society have always been fascinated with the mind, body, and spirit of African people. They have always been jealous of our ability to be so in touch with our surroundings, no matter what corner of the earth we are on. This is primarily due to the fact that we are the original people and have touched every part of the earth's globe, leaving behind in many cases, advanced civilizations that to this day cannot be explained or duplicated. However, many of us do not know this. Yeah, a few of us know about our greatness in Kemet and Nubia, but what about the rest of the world?

What about our presence in places like Europe, Asia, Australia, the pacific islands, or the Americas? What about our presence in civilizations such as Greece,

Rome, the Indus-Valley and more? Do we truly understand how special we are and how many gifts we have given to the world? Well, it's time to find out, let's go deeper on the black presence around the world and why other groups of people have always been fascinated with the aura that surrounds black people.

Europe

We already discussed in Volume I that the original modern-day Homo sapiens of Europe were the Grimaldi people. The Grimaldi people are an ancient African people that are believed to have migrated from the continent roughly 41,000 years ago, based on the Aurignacian layers they were discovered in. Since this discovery in 1901, scholars and historians have made comparisons in their physique to the modern-day Hottentots or the Khoekhoe people of South Africa. Further proof of this would come just seven years after the discovery of the Grimaldi men in the form of an ancient European sculpture called the Venus of Willendorf.

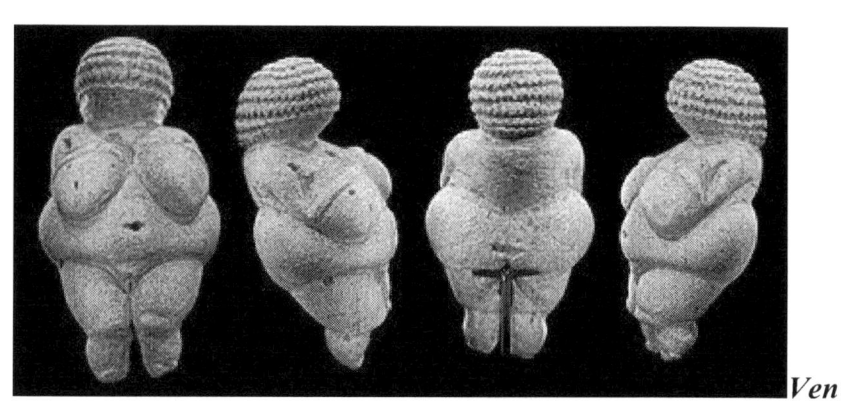

Ven us of Willendorf

Discovered in lower Austria in 1908 by Josef Szombathy, and his team of archaeologists, the Venus of Willendorf is a tiny sculpture roughly four and a half inches tall, that was carved out of limestone displaying what is believed to be a Grimaldi woman. After more than a century of speculation about the age of the sculpture, a revised analysis done by researchers in 2009 dated the sculpture to be roughly 30,000 years old, based on the archaeological layer in which it was found. Further examination of the sculpture over the years since its discovery led to many researchers concluding once again, that the ancient Grimaldi men were closely linked to modern day Africans. Swiss anthropologist Eugene Pittard, in his famous work *Les Races et l'Histoire* said, *"The Hottentots have what the scientists call 'pepper corn' hair; the Willendorf Venus has both steatopygia and pepper corn hair, which are two characteristics peculiar to the Hottentot....Each day Africa appears, more than ever, as having possessed the whole of our Paleolithic* (Old Stone Age) *and Neolithic* (New Stone Age) *civilizations".*

However, one should not be surprised by this, because anybody who knows their history will be able to see that there is a clear African presence in the more famous classical European civilizations. Take Ancient Greece for example, a civilization that is considered by most scholars to be one of the most influential on western culture and how we see the world today. First it is important to note and one must never forget that it was the Greeks who sat at the foot of the Kemites (Egyptians) to gain their knowledge, wisdom, and information. It was Hippocrates, a man who is considered even to this day as the "Father of Medicine", who was a descendant of a long line of students who learned from the teaching of Imhotep that was written down more than 2,200 years before Hippocrates was born. One of these students was Pythagoras, a man who many scholars accredit with discovering a formula to find the hidden side of a right triangle. You know that formula today as Pythagorean theorem or $a^2 + b^2 = c^2$.

Yet isn't it ironic that Pythagoras only developed this formula after spending years studying in Kemet? Something that many famous Greek writers like Herodotus and Isocrates spoke about in their works. Ancient Greek writers such as Antiphon even accredit Pythagoras with knowing how to speak Egyptian due to the amount of time he spent there. So again, the point is we must never forget that much of the knowledge, wisdom, and information that many praise the Greeks for having, only came after they studied us. Yet, with that

5

being said one must ask, who were the Greeks?

After all the traveling back and forth between Greece and Kemet that many Grecians took to study, one would think there would be a strong negroid strain among the Greeks as well, right? Especially when you consider that the Mediterranean Sea only separated the two mighty civilizations by less than 700 miles. To put that in perspective this is equivalent to the distance separating the cities of Atlanta, Georgia and Baltimore, Maryland, meaning as you might have guessed by now that the African presence in Ancient Greece was strong. So strong that famed Historian J.A Rogers once said *"In addition to their original Negro strain, the Greeks seem to have had a considerable number of unmixed Negros among them, principally as servants and soldiers. Black domestics were common"*. Greeks such as Alexander the Great became notorious for keeping Negroes in their armies.

In fact, one of Alexander's most trusted officers in his Macedonian army was a man name Cleitus, who on one occasion saved Alexander's life during the Battle of the Granicus. Cleitus is mentioned by Greek philosopher Plutarch and others as Cleitus Niger, meaning Cleitus the Negro. Moving on to two of the most famous Greek writers and storytellers Aesop and Sappho, were described as being negro as well according to many sources. Aesop for example in the anonymously authored *"Aesop Romance"* is described as being *"swarthy"* meaning dark skinned. Anthropologist J. H. Driberg, also asserted that, while *"some say he (Aesop) was a*

Phrygian... the more general view... is that he was an African".

Ancient *Delphi* thought by one antiquarian to represent Aesop

As stated, before the same could be said about Sappho. A woman who during her time was considered the greatest of all the poets. The great Roman poet Ovid made it clear that the ancients did not consider her white. Sappho is compared with Andromeda, daughter of a black Ethiopian king. A comparison that alluded to her blackness. One should also note the woman who she is being compared to, Andromeda and her significance in Greek history. For it was the beauty of Andromeda and her mother Cassiopeia, that the Greeks decided to name two of their most beautiful star constellations after them.

According to Greek mythology Andromeda was so alluring that the Greek gods grew jealous of her beauty, causing them to flood her kingdom and send the sea monster Cetus to kill her. Yet, she was saved by her demi-god hero Perseus making for not only popular Greek myth and folklore, but blockbuster Hollywood films in 1981 and 2010. Unfortunately, as is usually the case in these Hollywood films, Andromeda was portrayed as a white woman. Even though according to Greek mythology, she was an Ethiopian Queen, which is very telling of her physical characteristic, because when you study Greek literature you will find that the word Ethiopian is derived of the Greek word Aethiops which translates to burnt face. Therefore, most times the Greeks used the word just as much to describe a people's physical traits as where, they came from, which is why many Greek gods such as Zeus, Epaphus, Delphos and more have Ethiopian ties, according to Greek mythology.

Depiction of Andromeda by Bernard Picart, 1731

Moving along however, one should note that the

Romans just like their predecessors, had an African presence. Race mixing in Rome was very common and was spoken about by several influential writers of the time. St. Jerome said that Quintilianus a famous Roman educator had freed a Roman matron charged with adultery when she bore a black child. Martial, the great epigrammatist spoke about the tendencies of Roman matrons to cohabit with black men. He cited one example where a matron had borne seven children, none of which were her husband's but all of which were mixed.

Even the Roman scholar Pliny talks about products of black and white miscegenation in Rome. When speaking about the great Roman boxer Nicaeus, Pliny says, *"One certain example is that of the renowned boxer Nicaeus, born at Byzantium, whose mother was the daughter of adultery with a Negro. Her complexion was no different from that of the others (other white women), but her son Nicaeus appeared like his Negro grandfather."* These are just a few examples of the black presence in Ancient Rome when dealing with miscegenation, but we can go deeper. There were great playwriters such as Terentius Afer (Terence the African) who wrote many classical comedies that would later go on to inspire the likes of William Shakespeare and Phillis Wheatly.

Famous Roman historian Suetonius described Terentius as being *"fusco"* or dark colored. There were Roman emperors who were of African descent like Septimus Severus, who was born in Leptis Magna

(Libya) and whose father was of Punic ancestry. As well as Opellius Severus Macrinus, who was of a Berber ancestry from Mauretania Caesariensis (Algeria). There were even powerful and wealthy African women in Ancient Rome. Proof of this came with the 1901 discovery of the *"Ivory Bangle Lady"*, who's burial was found in York, England.

According to archaeologist her skeletal remains are dated to the second half of the fourth century towards the tail end of the Roman Empire. Also, further research done by the University of Reading's Department of Archaeology revealed a *"mixture of 'black' and 'white' ancestral traits"* and *"that she is of North African descent and may have migrated to York from somewhere warmer"*. This announcement by the University of Reading came as a shock to most, seeming as her burial was filled with artifacts and jewelry such as jet and elephant ivory bracelets, earrings, pendants, beads, a blue glass jug and a glass mirror. Items that not only proved she was of high status, but that African people in general were not just low-class slaves during the time of ancient Rome as many scholars portray.

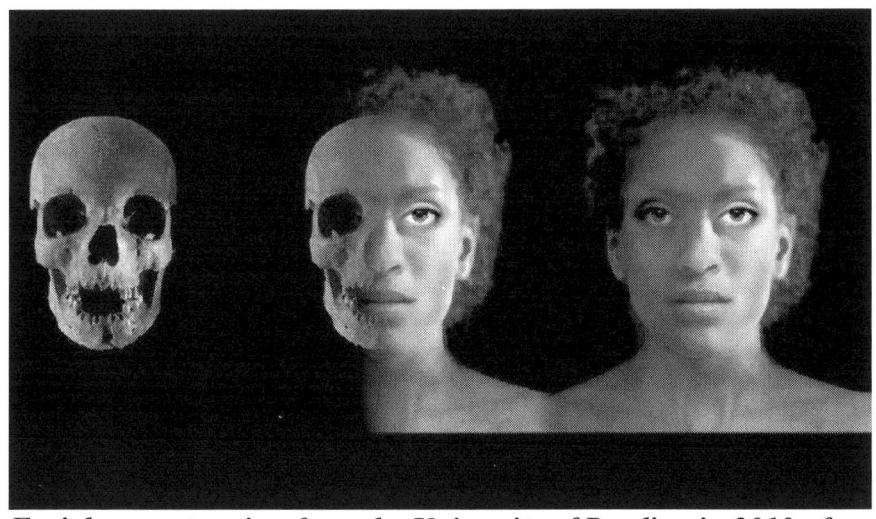

Facial reconstruction from the University of Reading in 2010 of Ivory Bangle Lady.

Asia

When we talk about the Black or African presence in ancient Asia, we must first start with the Negritos. The word Negrito is a Spanish word that means *"little black person"* and is used most often when referring to the native black people of Asia. These Negritos were the first inhabitants of Asia and were believed to be some of the first people to migrate out of Africa at least 70,000 years ago, facts that have been known for quite some time now as many current and past scientists, scholars and historians have spoken about in their works. One of the leading anthropologists in Europe during the early 1900's Giuffrida-Ruggeri, wrote in his book *"First Outline of a Systematic Anthropology of Asia"* in 1921 that *"the Negritos"* were the earliest inhabitants of India. Henri Imbert, a French anthropologist who lived in the Far

13

East, says in *"Les Negritos de la Chine"* written in the early 1900's, *"The Negroid races peopled at some time all the South of India, Indo-China and China"*. Imbert went on to say, *"The Negro element in Japan is recognizable by the Negroid aspect of certain inhabitants with dark and often blackish skin, frizzly or curly hair...The Negritos are the oldest race of the far east"*.

The Jarwa the Negritios of India

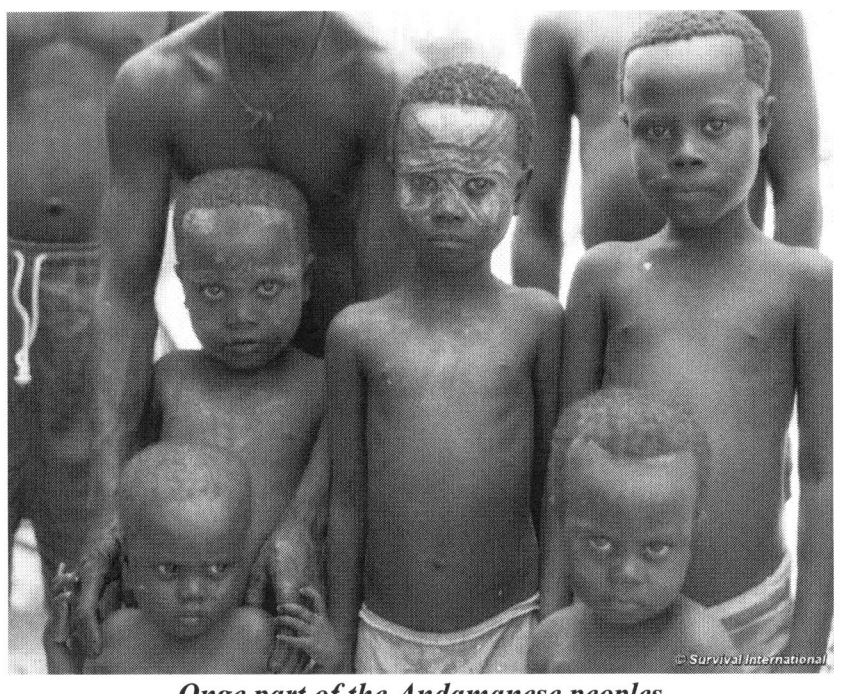

Onge part of the Andamanese peoples

Portrait of two Negrito women, each holding a baby, Philippine Islands

Recent genetic and archaeological evidence also supports past historians and scholars claims that the original Asians were black. The oldest human remains ever found in Asia belong to a black woman, scientists gave the name Tam Pa Ling. Upon the discovery in 2009 scientists confirmed that the 60,000-year-old skull had distinctive sub–Saharan African features, a fact that the media has since tried to silence. The negroid descendants of Tam Pa Ling can still be found in small pockets all over Asia till this day. For example, you have the Jarawa, the Onge, the great Andamanese, and the Sentinelese people, who now reside in the Andaman Islands of India.

These are an ancient people; studies of the Andamanese suggest that they are part of what is described as a relict Paleolithic population, descended from the first modern humans to leave Africa. Dr. Underhill, an expert on the genetic history of the Y chromosomes, said the Paleolithic population of Asia might well have looked as African as the Onge and Jarawa do now and that *"people with the appearance of present-day Asians might have emerged only later."* These later Asians that we describe now as being Mongoloid might in fact have very well pushed the once dominated Negrito populations out. The Spanish navigator Pedro Fernández de Quirós said on his expedition to the Philippines in 1595 *"In the Island of Luzon there are black men, who are said to be the aborigines of the land. They are called Pogotes and are retired on the island of Maragondon and other islands.*

For the Moors and other Indians occupy their lands, drive them away, and force those that remain into corners of the land where they now are. It may well be that, by reason of the invaders, the persecuted people have gone away to seek other settlements, until they came to New Guinea as the nearest place, and thence to the Solomon Islands and Santa Cruz."

The neighboring country of Taiwan has a similar oral tradition, speaking about how the Negrito populations were killed off. The Saisiyat, dance for three straight bonfire-lit nights every two years to remember the Negritos that they killed off thousands of years ago. Chu Fung-lu, master of ceremonies for the memorial held in Wufeng Village deep in the Taiwan mountains said when speaking about the dance *"There's a bit of guilt, so we're apologizing to them, we want them to protect us, to give us safety."* Yet, one should know that the Negrito's, were not the only black people this happened to in Asia. Understand there were different waves of black people who came to the continent over the years even after the Negritos.

Giuffrida-Ruggeri stated that after the Negritos there were the Pre-Dravidians, who were black like the Negritos but only taller, and then the Dravidians of today who are a mixture of negro, Aaryan and even a little mongoloid. These Dravidians would face a great amount of discrimination and abuse. Even today in south India they are still considered by many in the ruling class to be Dalits or the *"Untouchables."* Something that is

17

unfortunate because these Dravidians are living descendants of the Harappan people of the ancient Indus Valley civilization. The Indus Valley Civilization lasted from about 3500 B.C.E to 1700 B.C.E and stretched from the Persian Gulf to Mesopotamia.

The people who created and ran this civilization, the Harappan people were black. According to famed Historian Dr. Runoko Rashidi in his book the *African Star over Asia: The black presence in the East* he states *"We are equally certain that the founders of the Harappan civilization were black. This verifiable through the available physical evidence-skeletal remains, the eye-witness accounts preserved in the Rig Veda, artistic and sculptural remains, the regional survival of Dravidian languages, which are now being used in the decipherment of the Harappan script."* These black people were highly intelligent, building elaborate and complex cities that would rival ones of any ancient civilization. Many Indus Valley cities boasted impressive dockyards, granaries, warehouses, brick platforms, and protective walls to guard against flooding. These cities even included underground drainage systems that were the first of their kind.

In the city of Lothal for example in the southernmost tip of the Indus Valley, the main drainage sewer was 1.5 meters deep and 91 cm across and connected to many north-south and east-west sewers. It was made from bricks smoothened and joined together seamlessly. The expert masonry kept the sewer watertight. Drops at regular intervals acted like an automatic cleaning device. A wooden screen at the end of the drains held back solid wastes and liquids entered a cesspool made of radial bricks. Tunnels carried the waste liquids to the main channel connecting the dockyard with the river estuary. Even commoner houses had baths and drains that emptied into underground soakage jars.

The Dancing Girl, a prehistoric bronze sculpture made in approximately 2500 BCE in the Indus Valley Civilisation city of Mohenjo-daro.

However, as great as the Indus Valley Civilization was, it was honestly just the first of many black civilizations, empires, and kingdoms across Asia. For example, you have the Kingdom of Chenla that dated back to the middle of the 6th century A.D. Chenla covered a vast area including modern-day Cambodia, Laos, Thailand, and Vietnam. During Chenla's 200 plus year reign, its people built massive structures made of brick and stone, making them the first to do so in Southeast Asia. Many of the structures that were built are still standing today, like the Prasat Boram in Cambodia.

The kingdom of Chenla built on the knowledge, wisdom, and information that was left behind by their predecessors the Funanese. The Funanese built a kingdom known as the Kingdom of Funan that lasted from 1st century A.D. to the beginning of the Chenla Kingdom. Chinese historical documents speak on the Funanese as *"ugly and black. Their hair is curly."* The Chinese went on to describe the later Khmer men, builders of the most influential Southeast Asian kingdom Angkor as being *"small and black."* Something that was later confirmed by several scholars like Harvard's Roland Burrage Dixon who when referring to the ancient Khmers said that they were *"marked by distinctly short stature, dark skin, curly or even frizzly hair, broad noses and thick negroid lips."*

Pras at Boram in Cambodia

*Angkor Wat is a temple complex in **Cambodia** and the largest religious monument in the world by land area*

There was also a strong black or African presence in early Chinese civilizations. Three dynasties in particular stand out, the Shang, the Tang, and the Yuan. The Shang dynasty that was the earliest of the three dynasties, had a significant black presence, so much so that conquering Zhou described them as having *"black and oily skin."* The Tang dynasty that came next, displayed many statues of black or African people. Often referencing people with dark skin and spiral hair, similar to bantu knots. These statues can still be found around the world from the Victoria and Albert museum in London, to the Smithsonian museum in Washington D.C., representing some of the best artwork the Tang dynasty had to offer.

One can say the same about the Yuan dynasty, that

displayed black people in several paintings. Most notable of these paintings being the "tribute bearers" that was painted towards the end of the dynasty in 1350 A.D. The painting is now housed in the Asian Art Museum in San Francisco, and depicts four black men, one of which is of great prominence. All in all, family, I can go on for days about the black or African presence in Asia and would still not be able to cover it all. Therefore, I'll leave you with this. The great Dr. Ivan Van Sertima once said that it's one thing to say you were first, yet it's another to say what you did. This is the true mark of our greatness as a people, because not only were we first, but we were also the architects, the engineers, the educators, and civilizers. We were the gods that ruled Asia for thousands of years.

Australia, and the Pacific Islands

When it comes to the black or African presence in Australia and the Pacific islands, many will find that just like in Asia it cannot be denied. Although some scholars and historians when it benefits them will try to reclassify our brothers and sisters in these places to a completely different racial group, the proof of their black or African origins can be seen in all fields of study. As we spoke about in *"Voice of the Ancestors Volume I"* the Aborigines and the Torre Strait islanders made up the original inhabitants of Australia. Both of whom were a part of an out of Africa migration some 40,000 to 50,000 years ago.

While some have tried to give the illusion that these original inhabitants of Australia were dumb savages, who had no form of culture or civilization prior to the arrival of European colonists. The truth is several studies and newfound pieces of evidence discovered over the years, have helped to prove otherwise. Australian historian and anthropologist Inga Clendinnen for example, when speaking about the aboriginal culture in Australia prior to colonization said, *"They also developed steepling thought-structures -- intellectual edifices so comprehensive that every creature and plant had its place within it. They travelled light, but they were walking atlases, and walking encyclopedias of natural history."*

Indigenous writer Bruce Pascoe also spoke on the early inhabitants' complex system of agriculture and aquaculture in his book *Dark Emu: Black Seed: Agriculture or Accident?* He writes *"I came across repeated references to* (indigenous) *people building dams and wells, planting, irrigating, and harvesting seed, preserving the surplus and storing it in houses, sheds or secure vessels ... and manipulating the landscape."* One should also note when it comes to aquaculture that Australia is full of elaborate man-made dams and canals, used to control the water levels and trap aquatic life as these levels rise and fall. One of the most popular dams or canals is known as Budj Bim, located in southwest Victoria. The stones and foundations which remain today from the Budj Bim have been carboned dated to be over 6,000 years old, making the ancient engineering marvel of Budj Bim older than the Pyramids of Kemet, proving once again that although the original black inhabitants of

Australia might have been a simple people, they were highly intelligent and civilized.

Budj

Bim, a 6000-year-old Aboriginal engineering site

Moving on however, to the islands that surround and sit to the east of Australia, known as Melanesia, Micronesia, and Polynesia. One will find an even stronger black or African presence upon study and research, which is why we will start with Melanesia. Now it goes without being said that the most obvious thing that sticks out about these islands in particular, is the name it was given, Melanesia. Melanesia is a Greek word that literally means *"the black* (people) *islands"* a name given to it in 1832 by Jules Dumont d'Urville because of the dark-skinned natives that peopled the islands. The islands include four distinct countries Fiji (debatable), Papua New Guinea, Solomon Islands, and Vanuatu.

All of which include people who are dark or black skinned, have curly or kinky hair, and pertain typical Africoid facial features. In the Melanesian islands, especially in Solomon and Vanuatu, you will even see brothers and sisters who have rare traits not typically seen among black or African people. Traits such as blonde straight hair or reddish curly kinky hair are all physical characteristics that have left many of the world's top Geneticists puzzled and blown away, resulting in several theories about the origins and genetic makeup of our Melanesian brothers and sisters.

Two children from the Melanesian Island of Solomon

*A Fijian mountain warrior, photograph by **Francis Herbert Dufty, 1870s.***

Just like in Melanesian, Micronesia to the north, has a black or African presence, yet it is more refined and hidden. Micronesia which in translation means *"small islands"* is made up of thousands of islands and island chains, most notably being Caroline, Gilbert, Mariana, Marshall, Nauru, and Wake. Today these islands and island chains are inhabited with Micronesians having what some would call a Polynesian or mongoloid phenotype with fair/tannish skin and long straight hair. However, when one looks into the history of the

Micronesian island you will find out that this was not always the case. Several scientific voyagers of the past theorize that Micronesia just like Melanesian and Polynesia was once populated by an *"old black race"*. Although racist in their ways of reasoning, many of their theories hold some form of validity.

In 1756 Charles de Brosses, theorized that there was an 'old black race' in the Pacific who were conquered or defeated by the peoples of what is now called Polynesia, whom he distinguished as having lighter skin. Reinhold Forster theorized that a 'successive' migration of 'ancient Malays' had supplanted 'the aboriginal black race' in the pacific. French navigator Jean-François de Galaup de La Pérouse spewed the same theory upon visiting the islands in the 18th century, saying *"It appears to me evident, that all these different nations are the progeny of Malay colonies, which, in some age extremely remote, conquered the islands they inhabit.... But however, this may be, I am satisfied that the aborigines of the Philippine Islands, Formosa, New-Guinea, New Britain, the New Hebrides, the Friendly islands, in the southern hemisphere, and those of the Marianna and Sandwich islands in the northern, were that race of woolly-headed men still found in the interior of the islands of Luconia and Formosa. They were not to be subjugated in New Guinea, New Britain, and the New Hebrides; but being overcome in the more eastern islands, which were too small to afford them a retreat in the center, they mixed with the conquering nation. Thence has resulted a race of very black men, whose colour is still several shades deeper than that of certain families of the country, probably, because the latter have made it a point of honor to keep their blood unmixed. I was struck with these two very distinct races in the Islands of Navigators and cannot attribute to them any other origin".*

As a result of this in Micronesia one cannot find large groups of black people on the surface like in Melanesia, due to those ancient wars between the populations that pushed groups out. However, when one digs deep and looks at genetic markers such as haplogroups you will discover pockets of black or African people sprinkled within the Micronesian populations. A haplogroup is a genetic population group of people who share a common ancestor on the patriline or the matriline. According to Geneticist Tatiana M Karafet, certain haplogroups such as k2b1 are synonymous with Melanesians in Papua New Guinea and Negrito populations of southeast Asia such as the Aeta of the Philippines. Ironically enough the same haplogroup k2b1 is also significantly found among certain people in Micronesian.

Among the people of Guam 33% belonged to haplogroup k2b1, 63.64 % in the Marshall Islands, 61.5 % in Palau, 76.5 % among the Chuukese people of Chuuk and the surrounding islands, and 70% among the Pohnpeian people of the FSM. Meaning, although the black presence is not as visible in Micronesian as in Melanesian, it is there and the further back you go the more visible it becomes.

Nauruan warrior of Micronesia

Koror chiefs in 1915 from the island of Palau

Last but not least, we have arguably the most popular of the three major Oceania sub regions, Polynesia. Polynesia is a Greek word that translates to *"many islands"*, based on the fact that the region is made up of over 1,000 of them. Some of the islands include Easter Island, New Zealand, Samoa, Tonga, and even Hawaii, making the regions one of the most popular tourist destinations in the world. Yet, despite its popularity around the world, few know about the black or African presence throughout Polynesian history. In fact, people will often argue you down about the non – existence of it, attempting to make Polynesian a fixed race of people based on the region they live in, without acknowledging that within the group we call Polynesian you have different races, who come from different linages, and who have different physical characteristics.

Therefore, they may share the same culture, traditions and locations making them Polynesian but are of a different genetic makeup. The great historian J.A Rodgers, when speaking about the Polynesian people says, *"among whom are some pure blacks"* some *"are a mixture of negro, Caucasian, and Mongolian, with sometimes the last named predominant"*. Rodgers determined this based on a visit to the Museum of Natural History in Paris, France, where the exhibit held a large collection of life masks and photographs of the faces of the early pacific islanders from over a vast range.

Samoan Woman, 1910

Now some naysayers and critics will say, 'you

can't determine a person's race or lineage based strictly on how they look'. A comment I always find funny seeming that for the last 500 plus years, black folks around the world have been catching hell and put into racial categories based strictly on how they look. Yet, when we claim a people a part of our racial group based on the principles that have been laid out to us, phenotype, hair texture, skin color etc., we are the ones who are told you can't do that. Understand, this is what I like to call the moving of the racial goal post. Meaning, whenever it benefits the dominant society to categorize a particular group of people based on their physical appearance, then its ok. Yet, when it doesn't benefit them, it's not ok.

For example, when it comes to black-on-black crime the dominant society accepts the race of these so-called criminals based strictly on how they look. They treat us like one big Negro when it comes to crime or oppressing us, no matter where we were born, no matter the nationality we claim or car we drive. Yet, when the same group of black people begin to claim their history based on the racial categories that have been placed on them, then suddenly, the people who share the same phenotype, hair texture, and skin color aren't really the same people. They're not black anymore they are just Polynesian, they're not black they're just Indians, they're not black they're just Egyptians or my personal favorite in the words of James Henry Breasted, they're not black, they're just dark skin Caucasians, using very broad and ambiguous terms in order to try and move the racial goal post to their benefit, and our demise, putting us in a habit of jumping through hoops trying to prove the blackness of someone who in appearance is blacker than us.

Nonetheless, as black or African people we don't run from the truth we embrace it. So, when people ask for scientific evidence, we can give them that too. In the case of the Polynesians, we can prove the black or African presence using two scientific theories about how the Polynesians came to be. The two hotly debated theories are known as the *"Express Train"* and the *"Slow Boat"*, with most scientists and historians agreeing with one theory or the other. The *"Express Train"* theory brought forth in 1985, by archaeologist Peter Bellwood of the Australian National University in Canberra, proposed that the Lapita who would come to be the Polynesians, came out of southeast Asia. As the Lapita people left out, they passed through Taiwan, then the Philippines, before making a straight shot to the Polynesian islands.

The important thing to remember about the express train theory is it makes the claim that the Lapita people didn't begin to intermix with Melanesians until at least 500 years after being in the Polynesian islands. The *"Slow Train"* theory however argues a slower rate of migration for the Lapita people. Rather than originating from China or Taiwan 5,000 to 6,000 years ago and moving rapidly to Polynesia, the Lapita people have their origins in eastern Malaysia/Indonesia and western Melanesia. The "Slow Train" theory also argues that the migration took place much earlier, at over 30,000 years ago, citing that the genetics of the modern-day

Polynesian people are a direct reflection of the prehistoric migrants into Polynesia. Personally, in my educated opinion the "Slow Train" theory makes more logical sense based on the fact that according to the "Express Train" theory, the Lapita people hit the island of Fiji first. An island that is roughly 5,000 miles from southeast Asia and Taiwan.

Now if you're going to tell me that a people can move over 5,000 miles from the mainland of China to the Polynesian islands in a little bit over 300 years, then it would only make sense that Melanesian people on the island of Papua New Guinea for example, after being there 40,000 years could make the journey 2,500 miles to the same location. However, regardless of what scientific theory you choose, the science still backs up the fact that there was a black or African presence in the Polynesian islands at one point or another. In a 2016 Science Mag article siding with the *"Express Train"* theory entitled *"Game-changing' study suggests first Polynesians voyaged all the way from East Asia"* it stated, *"Polynesians today do carry a significant amount of Melanesian DNA"*. This was due to intermixing as stated earlier that started back as far as 2,500 B.C.E between Melanesians and the Lapita people. This happened throughout the many islands that make up Polynesia and can be seen in not just DNA, but literature and pictures as well.

Take Hawaii for example which make up multiple islands that sit farthest to the north of the Polynesian region, islands that make up one of the top tourist destinations especially among people in the United States. Yet, many of these tourists do not know about Hawaii's black past. They don't know that the last Queen, King, Prince, and Princess of the Kingdom of Hawaii were black. Their names were Queen Liliuokalani, King Kalakaua, Prince Leleiohoku II, Princess Ka'iulani, and they were the last royal family of the Kingdom of Hawaii.

Queen Liliuokalani the last Queen of the Kingdom of Hawaii

Queen Liliuokalani as a Teen.

Kalakaua last King of Hawaii

Leleiohoku II the last Prince of Hawaii

Kaiulani the last Princess of Hawaii

Based on appearance some were full blooded negroes like King Kalakaua others like Princess Kaiulani were mixed, seeing that her father was a Scottish businessman. The black presence in Hawaii however goes deeper than the last royal family, in fact it goes all the way back to the first. Starting with the first King and the founder of the Kingdom of Hawaii Kamehameha the Great, a man responsible for unifying all the islands and creating peace. He is depicted in several paintings most notably by famed German-Russian painter Louis Choris, as being black skinned and woolly haired.

Portrait of Kamehameha by Louis Choris ,1816

We also see notable descriptions of the Hawaiians in American and European literature starting with Kamehameha I's oldest son Kamehameha II. In 1824, Kamehameha II and his wife Queen Kamamalu, visited London, England, where they were described by the local London newspaper, *The Courier,* in great detail. The paper stated *"These Islanders are of a very large size. We only saw them sitting, but judging of their height from that posture, we should say the men are above six feet, and exceedingly stout. The females were equally fat and coarse made, and proportionately taller than the men.*

The whole party were of the darkest copper colour, very nearly approaching to black".

Portrait of Kamamalu Queen Consort of Hawaii attributed to John Hayter, 1824, Iolani Palace, Honolulu, Hawaii.

Another local London newspaper *Bell's* published an article referring to the Hawaiians as *"black looking Majesties"* while in the same breath referring to them as *"Savages"* due to their appearance. However, Kamehameha II and his Queen Kamamalu, would not be the last to receive racist remarks for their appearance. King Kalakaua and his sister Queen Liliuokalani, the last monarchs, would also receive their fair share of racist remarks, only this time from the American press. The *Columbus Journal* newspaper of Columbus, Nebraska and the *Northern Pacific Farmer* newspaper of Wadena, Minnesota, both made racist remarks aimed at Kalakaua's skin color during his travels to the United States. Same went for his sister Queen Liliuokalani, who was depicted by *The Judge* a US national newspaper, as a black savage with feathers in her head, the paper read *"Our good-natured country may allow this administration to give our market to England, sell our embassies to Anglomaniac dudes, and cause the reduction of wages to the European standard. But we draw the line at this".* Nothing more than a political dog whistle saying we might surrender to the mights of Britain, but not these Negroes. Because as J.A Rodgers stated, *"white southerners on the islands had a song which ran, you may call them Hawaiian, but they look like niggers to me".*

America

When it comes to the Americas, the only real question one should have is where do we begin? Therefore, let's start by saying the Americas are broken down into 3 main regions North, South and Central America, all of which have a unique history as it pertains to black or African people. This history can also be broken down in any of the given regions into 3 main categories, Indigenous, Exploration, and Captive History. The indigenous history deals with a time period before the slave trade prior to 1619 or 1526, in which the native people of the Americas had already settled on the land for thousands of years. The Exploration history deals with the black or African people who came engaging in trade as well as the ones who stayed and founded modern day American cities that we know today. Lastly, the captive history refers to the enslaved black people, most of whom were brought from west Africa to build the very foundations of the United States and many other countries.

Now it will be within the framework of these three categories in which I will be providing proof of a black or African presence in the Americas. Let's start with our indigenous presence in the Americas, something that is often hidden but cannot be denied. First it should be noted that many scholars and historians of the past both spoke about and pointed out the obvious black or African presence that laid within the Americas. For example, historian Carlos Marquez said in his work *"Estudios arqueologicos y etnograficos"* that *"it is [good] to report that long ago the youthful America was also a Negro continent"*. Leo Winer and Dr. Ivan Van Sertima also spoke extensively about the black or African presence in ancient America in their books *"Africa and the discovery of America"* and *"They came before Columbus"*. Both of these books were ground-breaking at the time yet dismissed by much of academia due to racial prejudice and stereotypes.

It should be noted that now just like back then, much of academia is still prejudiced towards the idea of there being a black or African presence among indigenous people of America. This is despite the overwhelming amount of evidence that has been brought forward to support the argument. The first piece of evidence or proof we have to support our argument are several firsthand eyewitness accounts of what the indigenous people of America looked like. The reason this is significant is because many of the native people we see today have little to no indigenous blood and are in fact five-dollar Indians, who became Native Americans or Indigenous people via paperwork rather than blood, a topic we touched on extensively in *Voice of the Ancestors* Volume II. Therefore, we cannot depend on the physical appearance of modern-day so-called natives to give us an accurate description of what the ancient ones looked like. So below I have listed five firsthand eyewitness accounts describing what the native people looked like from early European traders and explorers.

1.) In 1524, an Italian explorer name Giovanni de Verrazzano wrote a letter to King Francis describing the people of the Carolinas who he had seen on his travels. He said, *"The complexion of these people is black, not much different from that of the Ethiopians; their hair is black and thick, and not very long"*. Verrazzano in this letter also wrote about a boy who was saved by the natives after almost drowning at sea. Once the boy was returned to safety Verrazzano said *"This young man remarked that these people were black like the others, that they had shining skins, middle stature, and sharper faces, and very delicate bodies and limbs, and that they were inferior in strength, but quick in their minds"*.

2.) In 1602, an English explorer name

Bartholomew Gosnold, describes in a letter how the native people of Maine looked. He said, *"These people are of tall stature, broad and grim visage, of a black swart complexion."*

3.) In 1605, Captain George Weymouth on his voyage to the coast of Maine also spoke about and described four native women of the land. He said, *"They were very well favored in proportion of countenance, though colored black, low of stature, and fat, bare headed as the men, wearing their hair long: they had two little male children of a year and half old, as we judged, very fat and of good countenances, which they love tenderly."*

4.) In 1519, Antonio Pigafetta was a Venetian scholar and explorer who travelled with explorer Ferdinand Magellan during his voyage around the world. During this trip Antonio spoke about the native people of South America possibly Brazil. He said, *"And in this place there are boats, made from a tree all in one piece, which they call Canoe. They are not made with tools of iron (for they have none), but with stones like pebbles with which they plane and hollow the said boats. These boats hold thirty or forty men. And their paddles are made like iron shovels. And those who wield the paddles are black men all naked and shaved, and they look like enemies from hell."*

5.) In 1603, another English explorer name Martin Pring voyaged to the Northeast parts of the United States where he described the native people at Plymouth

Harbor. He said, *"These people in color are inclined to a swart (dark skinned), tawny (brownish) or chestnut color, not by nature but accidentally, and do wear their hair braided in four parts, and trussed up about their heads with a small knot behind."*

Now it is important to note as well, that all these accounts can be supported by early portraits of Native Americans done by artists such as Johann Ihle, Philipp Georg Friedrich von Reck, Louis Choris and more. Some of their portraits can be found below that display natives with black skin, curly kinky hair, and wide noses.

A Male Savage of Terra Del Fuego, 1795 by J. Chapman

"The supreme commander of the Yuchi Indian nation, whose name is Kipahalgwa," Georgia, 1736 painted by P. G. F. von Reck.

Louis Choris (German-Russian painter 1795-1828) Indians from the Bay area of San Francisco 1816

It should be noted as well, that not only was there a strong black or African presence in the Americas, but

there is an overwhelming amount of evidence to support
that the first Americans was black or African. Now to
prove this, one has to revisit the popular theory that the
so called first inhabitants of the Americas known as the
Clovis people were indeed the first Americans, who
crossed over the Bering strait 12,000 to 15,000 years ago.
The Clovis people are typically described by scholars and
historians as being Mongoloid, a stock we associate with
modern day Asians, and current Native Americans. Yet
archeological and biological evidence does not support
the theory of Mongoloid people being the first. For
example, in 2004 South Carolina professor/archaeologist,
Dr. Albert Goodyear, found an ancient campsite dating
back 51,700 years.

The discovery was located close to the Savannah
River in South Carolina less than 30 miles from the
Atlantic Ocean, where Dr. Goodyear and his team found
artifacts and burned plant remains in an ancient campfire
just four meters below the surface. Dr. Goodyear said,
*"This is the oldest radiocarbon-dated site of human
activity in North America."* So, it leaves the question if
the so called first inhabitants of the Americas, the Clovis
people came between 12,000 and 15,000 years ago, then
who did this campfire belong to? The answer is original
Negroid populations of the Americas who came by sea.
Now one of the biggest objections to this argument
comes from scholars and historians who say that ancient
people could not have traveled the seas since they did not
possess seafaring technology. A statement that has shown

to be not true based on the Bradshaw boat paintings in Australia that date back as far as 50,000 years, manmade tools found on the island of Crete dating back 130,000 years or Nubian and Chad pottery art that display ships which date back 5,000 plus years.

Quite frankly, to travel the seas, one would not even need modern day boating technology or navigation skills, just simply something that they could float on. This is because both the Atlantic and the Pacific Oceans have powerful currents that will float you from one continent to the other. Dr. Ivan Van Sertima in his book "They came before Columbus" talks about this as it pertains to the currents of the Atlantic saying *"currents that move with great power and swiftness from Africa to America. These currents may be likened to marine conveyor belts. Once you enter them you are transported from one bank of the ocean to the other."*

Proof of this came in 1952, when Alain Bombard a French doctor sailed from Morocco to Barbados in an inflated raft in just 52 days. This is the reason we see genetic connections even to this day between Native Americans and Africans. The Fuegians from South America for example, are genetically connected to the Khoisan people of sub-Saharan Africa, still sharing the same M 174 and D haploid groups, as the Benguela, Agulhas, and Brazilian currents can easily swing people from southern Africa to southern America.

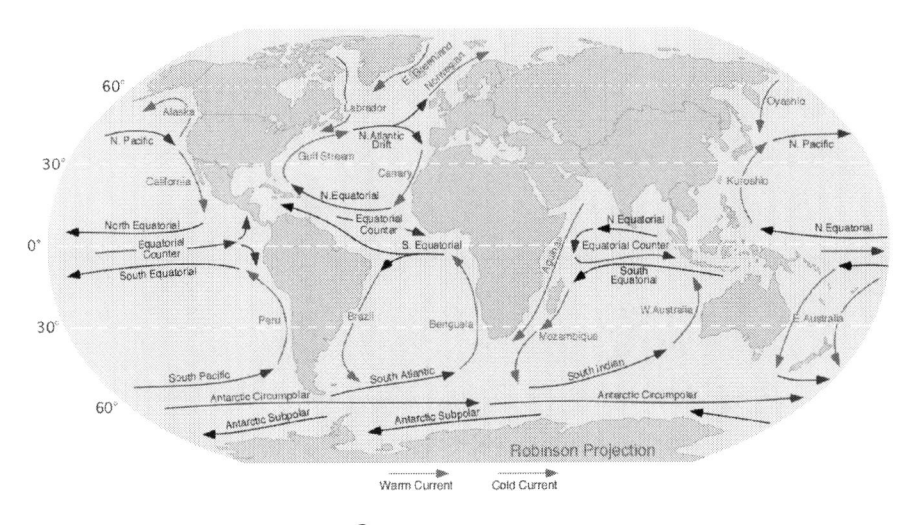

Ocean currents

It was because of these currents that black or African people from the east and west came to America to live, vacation, and engage in trade, influencing all of the major American civilizations such as the Olmec, the Mayans, the Aztec, and the Inca empires, while simultaneously helping to record, explore and build the land that we now call America. In fact (might put Jan Carew's Fulcrums of change origins of the name America) Explorers from the Mali empire such as Abubakari II might have made the first successfully recorded attempt to the Americas this according to his famed successor Mansa Musa. As Mansa Musa stated to Arab scholar Al-Umari *"He (Abubakari II) ordered two thousand boats to be equipped for him and for his men, and one thousand more for water and victuals. Then he conferred on me the regency during his absence, and departed with his men on the ocean trip, never to return*

51

nor to give a sign of life."

Interestingly enough, some 200 years later according to the poet Washington Irving, *"Columbus expected to find such people more to the south and southeast. He recollected that the natives of Hispaniola had spoken of black men who had once come to their island from the south, the head of whose javelins were of guanin or adulterated gold."* Columbus then sent a sample of the gold spear-tips back to Spain to be evaluated, where he surprisingly found out that the gold on the spear tips was not solid gold, but a metal alloy, meaning of several metals melted together. The formula used to make the spear-tip alloy was *"of 32 parts, 18 were of gold, 6 of silver, and 8 of copper."* This was identical to spears found in West Africa that were carried by medieval Moors and Mali warriors. Providing even more proof of a black or African presence in the Americas.

Our greatness in the Americas however never ended, even after the enslavement and transport of millions of west African and indigenous blacks, making up one of the worst holocausts in history, that unfortunately continues to play out to this day. Yet even during this time we still produced great explorers such as Jean Baptiste Du Sable, a Haitian who founded the city of Chicago now the third most populated city in the United States. Joseph "Black Joe" Hodge, a Foundational black American who was the first non-native to settle in the Buffalo, New York area, helping to establish a trading post between other settlers and the Native

Americans in the area. York the explorer, was a Foundational black American who accompanied Lewis and Clark on their expedition from coast to coast, helping to forge relationships with Native American tribes so they may pass through or trade. He was such an intracule part of the expedition that Clark named two locations after him, York's islands and York's dry Creek now known as Custer Creek both in Montana. California was named after a mythological black woman named Queen Califia who fascinated the Spanish people so much that upon them arriving at the newfound land they named it California as a tribute to her.

Ironically enough the last governor of California under Mexican rule was a black man named Pio Pico, who during his day was one of the wealthiest men in the country. Tuscaloosa, Alabama home to one of the most prestigious college football programs in the nation the Alabama Crimson Tide is named after Chief Tuscaloosa who's name literally means *"The Black Warrior."* We can go on and on from Daniel Hale Williams, who was the first man in the United States to perform open heart surgery to Elijah McCoy, a master inventor who held over 50 patents for his numerous inventions. Even Foundational Black Americans like Bass Reeves who during his career as a U.S. Marshall locked up and arrested over 3,000 people. His story would later be betrayed in Hollywood as the famous hit show the Lone Ranger. Yet, the point is the black or African presence is so significant and important to America that without it there would be no America.

Bass Reeves the real "Lone Ranger"

Daniel Hale Williams first doctor to perform open heart surgery in U.S.

Africa

Last but not least, we have Africa, a place that

many would consider the garden of Eden for not only humanity but civilization as a whole. Over the past several decades we've had many scholars within our community debunk the myths and bring to light the truth of Africa in a way that was much needed. From Dr. Yosef Ben Jochannan to Dr. John Henrik Clarke, from Cheikh Anta Diop to J.A. Rodgers and Dr. Ivan Van Sertima, all of these Ancestor's work should be applauded and never forgotten, for they set the foundation for the knowledge, wisdom, and information we know today. Which is also why in this section I will try to stay away from talking about Nile Valley Civilizations as much as possible, because although we love them and never get tired of reading about them, they have been the most documented. Especially in the extensive works of the Master teachers I mentioned above.

Therefore, in this section I will discuss great west, central, and south African civilizations that are almost always overshadowed or never spoken about. Yet, before I do that I want to discuss and talk about the word Africa, because over the past few years the origin or etymology of the word has been hotly debated. I've heard several people within our community say things like *"You shouldn't call yourself or refer to yourself as African because Africa got its name from a White man"*. Untrue phrases like this have become popular within our community, as a result causing a lot of people to disassociate with the continent altogether. So, let's correct the wrongs and talk about it, after all, did Africa really get its name from a white man?

Now let me first say that the base of this argument circulates around a man name Publius Cornelius Scipio Africanus. A man who was a white Roman General during the second Punic War, in which he defeated Hannibal and took over Carthage. Because of this, many people have jumped to the conclusion that Scipo Africanus named Africa after himself, but this is not true. In fact, it was the opposite. Publius Cornelius Scipio Africanus got his name from Africa, and although many scholars and historians debate over the true origin, most agree it is an indigenous word that came from people on the continent.

Now what do I mean? His true birth name is simply Publius Cornelius Scipio, a name he received after his father. His last name Africanus is what is known in Roman literature as a cognomen meaning essentially a nickname. He received this nickname because of his military victory against Hannibal and the people he was fighting in North Africa known as the Afri or Afer people. These people called their land Afri land, a phrase the Romans combined and called Afri-ca. This was a popular thing to do amongst the Romans, whenever military victories were achieved by a particular individual.

Publius Africanus had a brother named Scipo Asiaticus because of the military victories he achieved in western Asia. Germanicus Julius Caesar received his cognomen of Germanicus for defeating the Germanic tribes in now modern-day Germany. So again, more cases of Roman Generals naming themselves after the people or land they conquered. Furthermore, proving that the name was already there and amongst the indigenous people in the area. In fact, when it comes to the word Africa, the origins of the word might go as far back as Kemet.

According to Egyptologist Gerald Massey in his book *"Ancient Egypt: The Light of the World Volume I and II"* he says, *"I began my study in 1870, with the idea, which has grown stronger every year, that the human race originated in equatorial Africa."* Massey found that in the Ancient Kemetic language *"Af-rui-ka"* means *"to turn toward the opening of the Ka."* The Ka is the energetic double of every person and the *"opening of the Ka"* refers to a womb or birthplace. Therefore, Africa would be, for the Kemites, *"the birthplace"*.

Now that we've gotten that out the way let's discuss the great civilizations and city states of west, central, and south Africa as promised. Below I have listed 10 empires or city states that we should all know, that is not in the Nile valley region.

1.) The Ghana Empire (300 A.D. - 1235 A.D.)

The first of these empires to come about was the Ghana empire. The Ghana or Wagadu Empire as it is sometimes called, flourished in West Africa from roughly 300 A.D.- 1235 A.D. because they were excellent traders of the desert sands. The domestication of the camel helped them to export larger quantities of salt, copper, gold and more, to nations across west Africa, making for a very long sustaining and wealthy empire that set the very foundation for the west African empires that would follow. The Ghana empire was so influential that nearly all the historic descriptions we have, come from Arabic scholars who came and visited from around the world. Abu Ubaydallah al-Bakri for example was an Arab scholar from Cordoba, Spain who visited the Ghana empire in 1068. During this visit, he recorded that amazing city and the people, saying *"The city of Ghana consists of two towns situated on a plain. One of these towns, which is inhabited by Muslims, is large and possesses twelve mosques, in which they assemble for the Friday prayer. There are salaried imams and muezzins, as well as jurists and scholars. In the environs are wells with sweet water, from which they drink and with which they grow vegetables...The houses of the inhabitants are of stone and acacia wood. The king has a palace and several domed dwellings all surrounded with an enclosure like a city wall...On every donkey-load of salt when it is brought into the country their king levies one golden dinar and two dinars when it is sent out. The nuggets found in all the mines of his country are reserved for the king, only this gold dust being left for the people. But for this the people would accumulate gold until it lost its value... The king of Ghana when he calls up his army, can put 200,000 men into the field, more than 40,000 of them archers. "* However, despite this account and several others by Arab scholars, many have continued the same hate and envy toward west African civilizations as they do towards Nile valley civilizations. Denying they existed all together or turning the Ghana empire for example white. Yet the fact is as Arabs would say during the time, the region that made up the Ghana empire was *"Bilad al-Sudan"* aka *"land of the Blacks."*

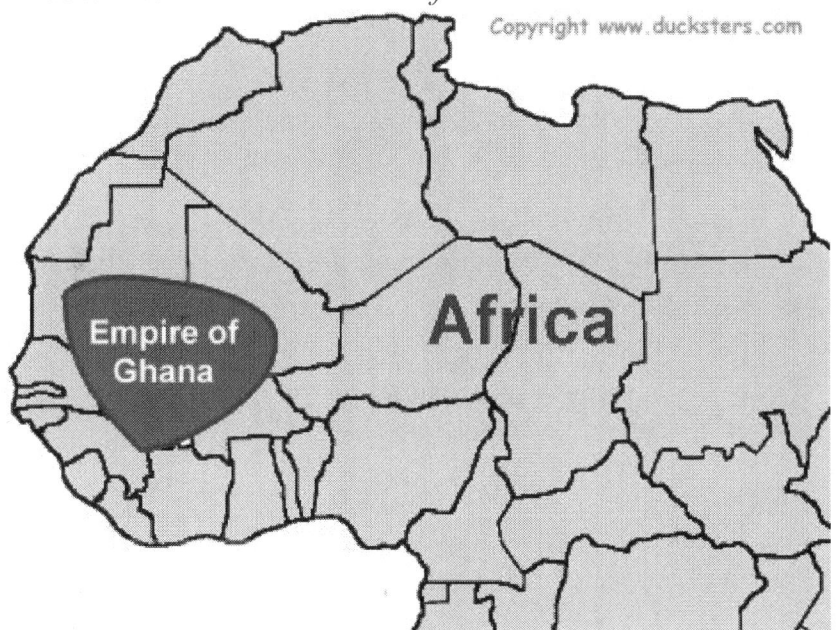

Empire of Ghana (Green Area)

2.) *The Mali Empire (1230 A.D. - 1600 A.D.)*

The Mali empire is an empire that would pick up where the Ghana empire fell off, as the two nearly ran in succession with one another. From 1230 A.D. - 1600 A.D. the Mali Empire would become world renowned for not only its massive cities and schools but also its unseen amount of wealth and resources. The empire would stretch across west Africa touching eight modern day countries including, The Gambia, Guinea, Guinea-Bissau, Ivory Coast, Mali, Mauritania, Niger, and Senegal. The first king of Mali was King Sundiata Keita who would take the title "Mansa" or "King of Kings." The great King would go on to establish the "Kouroukan Fouga" one of the earliest constitutions in the world. The "Kouroukan Fouga" contained a preamble of seven chapters advocating social peace, education, the abolishment of slavery and more. This would set the foundation for the empire becoming one of the most powerful in the world. Creating prominent and charismatic figures such as Mansa Musa the richest man to ever live or Ahmed Baba a prolific writer and prominent Islamic scholar. While at the same time Mali housed a world class educational system that held nearly 700,000 documents. The university of Timbuktu was considered the best college of its day where scholars from all over came to learn.

Voice of the Ancestors III

The Great Mosque of Djenné

3.) *The Songhai Empire* (1464 A.D. -1591 A.D.)

The Songhai Empire is what many would call the last of
the great west African civilization and essentially ran
concurrent with the tail end of the Mali empire. In fact, it
was an event that took place during the powerful rule of
Mansa Musa that gave birth to the Empire. After Mansa
Musa famed trip to Mecca, he returned home only to find
that a city within his empire name Gao had been
recaptured by local rebels. After forcing the King of the
rebellion to surrender, Mansa Musa took both of his boys
to ensure the people's continued compliance. The young
princes Ali Kolon and Suleiman Nar were treated well
but forced to subdue their own people in the city of Gao
as soldiers. This made Ali Kolon grow very bitter and
angry until he eventually made a vow to escape with his
brother to free their people in Gao. When the time came,
they strategically fled back to Gao where they would lead
a war against Mali, over the years slowly unifying the
local people and weakening Mali. During this time Ali
Kolon changed his name to Sunni Ali and established the
Sunni Dynasty. These rulers of the Dynasty would
magnify the power of Gao and turn the powerful Songhai
nation into the Songhai empire, where for the next 100
plus years Songhai would be ruled by warrior kings with
the names Sunni and Askia. Their warrior rulers used
highly skilled horsemen and war canoes making their
ability to utilize any terrain to their advantage

unparalleled. Without question the most famous of the warrior kings was a man named Sunni Ali Ber, not to be confused with the prince who ran away. Sunni Ali Ber was a military genius who put fear in the heart of his enemies. Abdul-Rahman al-Sa'di says about him, *"He surpassed all the previous kings in his bravery. His conquests were many, and his fame extended from the rising to the setting of the sun. If it is the will of god, he will be spoken for a long time."*

Recreati

on of the great Sunni Ali Ber

4.) Carthage (814 B.C. - 146 B.C.)

Carthage was an ancient African city-state in modern day Tunisia that at its height was the largest, most affluent, and powerful political entity in the Mediterranean. Tribute and tariffs regularly increased the city's wealth on top of the lucrative business in maritime trade. The city's harbors were immense, with 220 docks, and gleaming columns. There were two harbors, one for trade and the other for warships, which operated constantly in resupplying, repairing, and outfitting vessels. The Carthaginian trading ships sailed daily to ports all around the Mediterranean Sea while their navy, supreme in the region, kept them safe and, also, opened new territories for trade and resources through conquests as the Carthaginians built their empire. The descendants of the Phoenicians, Carthaginians were a very diverse racial group, having people from many different cultures and backgrounds from around the Mediterranean. Meaning despite popular belief Carthage had a strong black or African presence within it. Famed 18th century German geographer and ethnographer Friedrich Ratzel says regarding these inhabitants of North Africa,*"Negroes crossed the Alps with Hannibal and fell at Worth beside McMahon. Whatever their original nature may have been, all this population must have been alloyed with a strong Ethiopian element...The entire Semitic and Hamitic population of Africa, has, in other words, a mulatto character which extends to the Semites outside Africa."* The great military general Hannibal was black as well as he was featured on several coins during the time depicting his negroid features. This was due to the tremendous effort, he put forth against the mights of the Roman army during the Punic wars. A war that unfortunately led to the downfall of Carthage.

Hannibal Barca Coins

5.) Nok Civilization (1500 B.C. to 200. A.D.)

Some might argue that the Nok civilization wasn't really a civilization but rather a culture, yet despite this no one will argue against the innovative people living in this area. Located in southern West Africa (now modern-day Nigeria) from 1500 B.C. to 200. A.D. these ancient Nigerians would become some of the greatest sculptors and iron smelters in the world. The majority of the Nok figurines they created date back to the Middle period and are easily distinguishable by their large heads and facial features. These facial figures typically depicted important political people or ancestors based on the fact that they wore prestigious forms of decoration. Complete figurines number in the thousands ranging in size from 300 millimeters to one meter with many being housed in Museums and Art Galleries around the world. Yet as stated before, the Nok civilization was multi-talented. We see evidence of this from smelt and use iron in unique ways. The remains of perhaps 13 iron-smelting furnaces were discovered at Taruga alone. Durable iron tools such as hoes, hand-axes and cleavers were put to good use to boost agricultural efficiency, allowing farmers to grow cereals like sorghum and unique vegetables like pumpkins, making for a very vibrant and innovative ancient west African culture.

One of thousands of Nok figurines

6.) *Kilwa (900 A.D. - 1500 A.D.)*

The ancient city state of Kilwa also known as Kilwa Kisiwani, was the Miami of its day. Located in East Africa on the beautiful Swahili coast of Tanzania, Kilwa became a notorious city state for trade. Kilwa dominated the import/export business of goods coming in and out of

Africa and to Arabia, Persia, and India. The residents of Kilwa saw the fruits of this trade and many were extremely wealthy, especially because their south outpost of Sofala was a huge port of Zimbabwe gold. Kilwa's architecture was also top of the line as it featured several stone buildings and Mosques. Most famous of the structures probably being the Great Mosque of Kilwa, that was built including 16 bays, supported by nine pillars, originally carved from coral stones. 13th century intellectual Ibn Battuta also said this about the city upon his visit *"We ... traveled by sea to the city of Kilwa...Most of its people are Zunuj, extremely black...The city of Kilwa is amongst the most beautiful of cities and most elegantly built... Their uppermost virtue is religion and righteousness, and they are Shafi'i in rite."* Researcher Edward John Pollard also teaches us that although trade connections with the Arabian Peninsula as well as India and China influenced the growth and development of Kilwa, and, though there are Islamic words and customs that have been adapted to the culture, the origins are African.

Ruins from the Great Mosque of Kilwa

7.) *Kingdom of Mutapa (1450 A.D. - 1750 A.D.)*

The Kingdom of Mutapa was a Kingdom located at the southern tip of Africa that at one time covered the modern-day countries of Zambia, Zimbabwe, Mozambique, and South Africa. What made the Kingdom of Mutapa so unique was their ability to fight off foreign invaders like the Portuguese for so long. They were able to do this by engaging in a powernomics concept, using their wealth to buy political and military power amongst the people. For example, the Gold and silver was made into bracelets by local craftsmen, then was used as gifts that were given by the king to officials and regional governors to ensure their loyalty. Trade was centrally regulated, with weights and measures controlled by the court. All things were regulated from the import/export business to "the volume of local produce on the international market" to maintain "a favorable balance of trade." Everything was to make sure they controlled all levels of activity on a domestic and international level, becoming essentially too big to fail. However, the fall and collapse came from in-fighting amongst the Mutapa people, allowing the Portuguese as a result to divide and conquer.

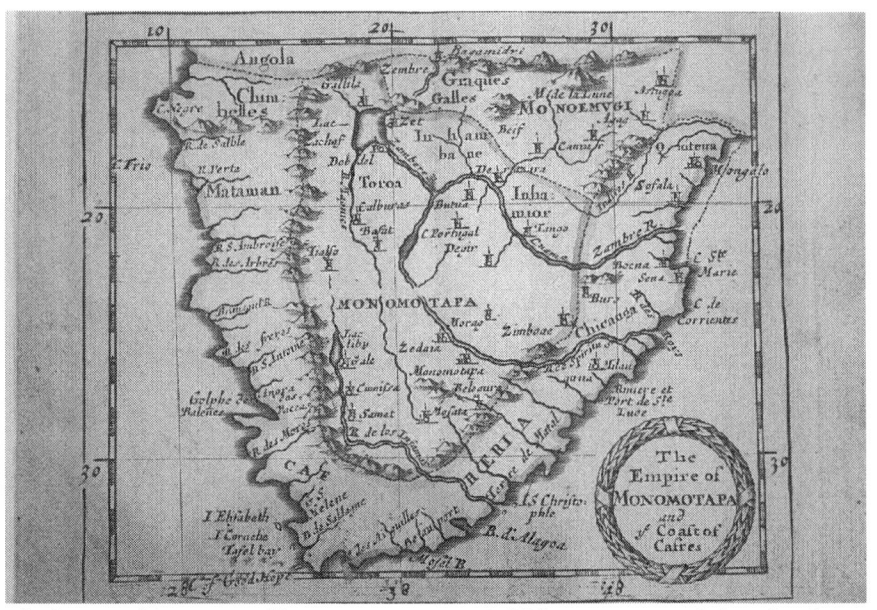

A sixteenth-century Portuguese map of Monomotapa lying in the interior of southern Africa.

8.) *Ajuran Empire* *(Early 13th century A.D. - Late 17th century A.D.)*

The Ajuran Empire is an empire that is hardly ever spoken about and that's probably because it is overshadowed with all the greatest the Nile valley civilizations had to offer. Yet this later Northeast African empire was special in its own right, mainly due to its architectural and military achievements. Located in the southern region of Somali the Ajuran Empire became one of the few Northeast African empires to defeat a European power on the sea. Through a strong centralized administration and an aggressive military stance, the Ajuran Empire successfully resisted an Oromo invasion from the west and a Portuguese incursion by sea from the east during the Gaal Madow and the Ajuran-Portuguese wars. Because of their military achievements they were able to build a long-standing legacy in the region leaving several cities, castles and fortresses built by Ajuran engineers. All was funded by a flourishing economy with major agricultural towns, located at key points on the Shebelle and Jubba rivers. This allowed some of the busiest medieval trade routes to flow right through the Ajuran Empire giving them access to clients from Africa to east Asia. All in all making for a very wealthy empire.

The Fakr Ud Din mosque, built in Mogadishu around the time it fell under the control of the Ajurans.

9.) The Kingdom of Zimbabwe (1100 A.D. - 1500 A.D.)

The Kingdom of Zimbabwe was a pre-colonial Kingdom in southern Africa that dominated the ivory and gold trade from the interior to the southeastern coast of Africa. Zimbabwe means *"House of Stones"* something that is evident when one looks at the structures that were built there. The Kingdom is most famously known however for its capital city Lusvingo aka Great Zimbabwe, which holds the largest stone structure in pre-colonial southern Africa. The Great Zimbabwe consists of several sections, with walls built without mortar, relying on carefully shaped rocks to hold the wall's shape on their own. These walls in some areas of the structure tower as high as 33 feet and housed as many as 20,000 people at a time, making it a very influential trade center of its day. European explorers and scholars were so amazed upon seeing it that they claimed it couldn't have been built by Africans, and instead thought it had been built by non-African people. See, it was Kingdoms like Zimbabwe that powered other African empires like Kilwa and Sofala and led to the succession of others such as Mutapa and Butua, one of the main reasons why in 1986, the ruins of Great Zimbabwe were designated a United Nations Educational, Scientific and Cultural Organization World Heritage Site, for the impact it left.

The Great Zimbabwe ruins

10.) <u>Kingdom of Kongo</u> (Late 14th century A.D. - Early 19th century A.D.)

The Kingdom of Kongo is another one of the many African Kingdoms that leaves African enthusiasts amazed. Located on the west coast of Central Africa, the Kingdom of Kongo prospered in the trade of ivory, copper and unfortunately slaves. At its peak in the 15th and 16th century, the kingdom controlled some 150 miles of river coast to the North and South as well as spread some 250 miles into the interior of central Africa up to the Kwango River. As the Kingdom amassed such fortunes due to territory and trade, the cities within its domain also flourished. The kingdom became one of the biggest in the region, at its height housing around 3.9 million people inside the borders of its walls that surrounded the kingdom. The houses that sat inside the wall were made of mud brick. There was also a foundation layer of stones upon which these bricks were placed, to prevent moisture from climbing up through the ground. There was even a fireplace installed in the houses in order to keep them dry and warm. All of this made for very sturdy and durable houses. Another major achievement of the Kongo Empire was its dedication and encouragement of art. The most talented sculptors were often felicitated in national festivals by the Manikongo, despite the greatness of the Kingdom of Kongo fighting amongst each other was once again the downfall. Around 1568 Kongo was temporarily overrun by rival warriors from the east known as the Jagas. Álvaro I Nimi a Lukeni was able to restore Kongo but only with Portuguese assistance. In exchange, he allowed them to settle in Luanda and create the Portuguese colony that became the earliest region of Angola. The rest was history as the Portuguese slowly but surely began to gain a tighter and tighter grip on the kingdom.

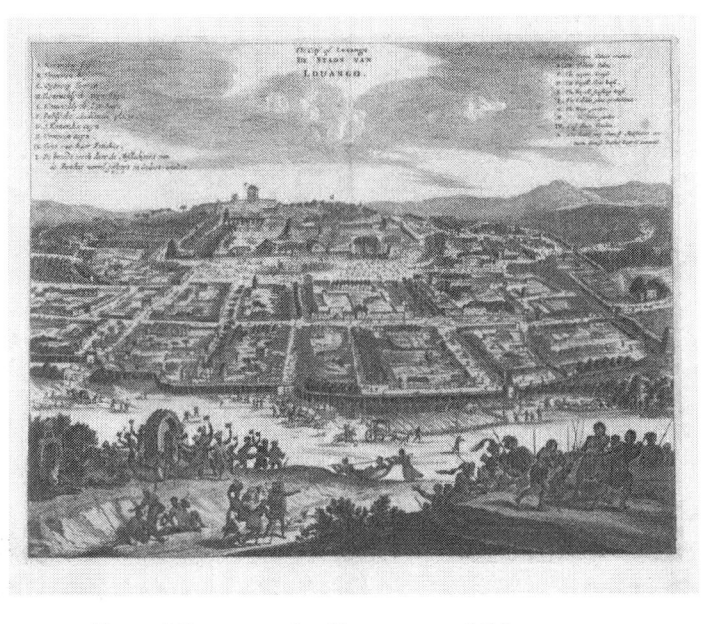

City of Loango, in Kongo ca. 17th century

Bonus

<u>The Kingdom of Madagascar</u> (16th century A.D. - 19th century A.D.)

<u>Kingdom of Dahomey</u> (1600 A.D. -1904 A.D.)

<u>Garamantes</u> (1000 B.C. - 600 A.D.)

Honestly family, I can go on and on for days about hidden African civilizations, empires, and city states without mentioning the great ones in the Nile Valley, because the facts are the Nile Valley was just one small piece of the legacy we left behind, which is a testament of our greatness as a people, a greatness they never want us to discover again. We must never allow our enemies to regulate our history to one specific country, region or even continent. Which is why it's up to us to tell our own story, for that is all "His-Story" is.

Conclusion

In conclusion if you haven't noticed already, we are a very unique and special group of people. A people who was not only the first to arrive but the first to civilize. This is something that can never be taken away from us because it is us. We are living examples of the greatness that came before and after and that greatness cannot be relegated to a specific time or place for it is everlasting and eternal. Therefore, sit-up and walk with your head held high for it is not a place you haven't been or obstacle you haven't overcome. You are a God and gods don't die they multiply.

My Mother Said

My mother said she was African, no matter where she stood, you could take her feet off African soil, but you couldn't take her African good.

My mother said her mother, was the mother of civilization. You could take her name you could cause her shame, but you couldn't take that salutation.

My mother said that I was royalty, Crown Prince of the mother lands, she said I wasn't considered much over here, but back home I was truly grand.

My mother said my melanin is a gift and I should be

proud, she said darkness of hue is god's gift to you, your personal protective shroud.

My mother said my hair like Sampson represented strength, one shouldn't hide their race pride because the power's in the lock not the length.

My mother said many things and most I put on a shelf, but one thing is clear, I can still hear, son learn to love yourself.

My mother said Jesus was African, Noah was African, she said Moses was African looked nothing like Charlton Heston.

My mother said everybody from the Island's African. Dominican Africans, Puerto Rican Africans, Haitian Africans, Jamaican Africans.

My mother said everybody on this planet came from Africa originally that's what my mother said.

My mother said many things and most I put on a shelf, but one thing is clear I can still hear, son learn to love yourself.

-Ty Gray El

Part. 2

Black Economic Empowerment: Recreating A Black Wall Street

How are you going to talk Black Power, without the Black dollar?

-Dr. Umar Johnson

Introduction

We discussed in *Voice of the Ancestors VI* the three keys to liberation, which were knowledge of self, black economic empowerment, and Military science. Well in this section we will go even deeper, specifically as it concerns black economic empowerment. Reason being when we look at black or African people from broader world perspective, we will find that we in America have a unique situation compared to black people in other parts of the world. In that we are essentially participating in our own holocaust.

For example, according to research by the University of Georgia's Selig Center for economic growth, in 2016 the purchasing power of blacks in America reached 1.2 trillion. That 1.2 trillion in spending power was more than countries such as Egypt, Nigeria, South Africa, Morocco, Angola and more. In other words, we as blacks in America has more spending power than any country in Africa, making us economically speaking, the most powerful black nation on earth. Now you would think that with all this spending power we would spend our money on the guns. By guns I mean your real estate, your stocks, your bonds, and other investment instruments. Assets that over time work for you and appreciate in value.

However, we as black or African people do not spend our money on the guns, we spend our money on the butter. The butter being the cars, clothes, alcohol, and other items that depreciate over time. Statistics show that we as a people on average are 6 times more likely than white people to buy a Mercedes, and the average income of a black who buys a Jaguar is about 1/3 less than that of a white purchaser, according to Earl Graves, *Black Enterprise Magazine*. Yet on the flip side of that, we are the poorest race of people in America, speaking per household. With the average black family only having a net worth of just over 11,000. Why is it that we as black people are 6 times more likely to buy a Mercedes Benz then a white person, or that our income is one third a white purchaser of a Jaguar?

The answer is simple, and we see it all the time as black or African people, that we are in love with symbolism. As Dr. Umar Johnson preaches all the time, *"one thing we know about oppressed people, when you can't enjoy true freedom, you surround yourself with the symbols of that freedom"*. As a result, it has caused us to create bad habits. We are illiterate in terms of financial literacy. The way we are spending our money is crazy. In 2016 for example we spent 2 billion dollars on athletic, 4 billion dollars on liquor and alcohol and 600 million on fast food.

While at the same time a quarter of black people in America had no assets other than a car, compared to just 6% of white Americans without assets other than a vehicle. We cannot continue hollering black power or black lives matter and then not talk about the black dollar. It's about priorities, and our priorities in 2021 are messed up. That's why in this section we are going to discuss some of the tools we need to build an economic power system, in order to move forward in our quest for black liberation and salvation.

Banking Black

I like to start this conversation on black economic empowerment at the bottom because most of us without any knowledge on financial literacy or powernomics must crawl before we can walk. The first step to crawling, speaking in terms of black economic empowerment, is banking black. This is a very simple but yet important step in terms of empowering our community. Any economist will tell you the bank is key to the stability and the success of any given community. It is a simple way for members of the community to help empower their self along with the community as a whole, with little to no risk. The reason being is that the bank is responsible for issuing out the loans for houses, schools, businesses, hospitals and much more.

All-important entities that are needed to fuel and keep our dollar circulating within our community. Take a bank like East West Bank for example, a Chinese based bank that is still pretty new historically speaking. Opening its doors for the first time in 1973. Due to the overwhelming flow of Chinese immigrants at the time, East West Bank set out to be the first federally chartered saving institution focused primarily on serving the financial needs of Chinese Americans in Los Angeles.

Keywords being "*focused primarily on Chinese Americans*".

This Focus led to the attention of Chinese Americans and the importance of banking Chinese. Today East West Bank has grown and flourished to a full-service commercial bank with over 125 locations in key cities in the US and greater China. During this 40-year period increasing their management assets to just over 50 billion. This money in return was then able to be distributed back to the Chinese community in order to create a strong economic base among their people. That's why if you notice, in all of these cities where East west bank is located, Houston, Atlanta, Los Angeles, New York etc., there is always a Chinatown or a flourishing Chinese community.

I was born and raised in Atlanta in a predominantly black neighborhood. However, in my neighborhood you will find that half if not the majority of the businesses are owned by Chinese people. The reason is that they have access to immediate capital from Chinese Banks like East West, enabling them to get a $50,000 business loan at a good to reasonable interest rate. Either that or they come in with a line of credit from their home country. The Chinese community is not the only one that bank with their own. The Jewish community, Arab community, East Indian community and so on, all bank with their own. Yet, let me be clear, I'm not at all telling you to blame these communities for banking with their own people, because what they did was smart, they understand what Dr. Claud Anderson calls powernomics.

However, I am mad at us for not engaging in a powernomics concept as well, by banking black. See, contrary to popular belief and misconception in the black community, we do have black Banks and Credit Unions. Here's is a list of them all as of January 29th, 2021.

Black-Owned Banks: State-by-State Breakdown

Alabama

- **OneUnited Bank:** Multiple ATM locations[21]
- **Alamerica Bank:** Birmingham[22]
- **Citizens Trust Bank:** Birmingham and Eutaw[23]
- **Commonwealth National Bank:** Mobile[24]
- **Liberty Bank:** Montgomery and Tuskegee[25] [26]
- **Hope Credit Union:** Montgomery[27]

Alaska

- **OneUnited Bank:** Multiple ATM locations[21]

Arizona

- **OneUnited Bank:** Multiple ATM locations[21]

Arkansas

- **OneUnited Bank:** Multiple ATM locations[21]
- **Hope Credit Union:** College Station, Little Rock, Pine Bluff, and West Memphis[27]

California

- **OneUnited Bank:** Multiple ATM locations, in addition to the Corporate Office and Crenshaw Branch, as well as the upcoming Compton

Branch[21]
- **Broadway Federal Bank:** Los Angeles[28]

Colorado
- **OneUnited Bank:** Multiple ATM locations[21]

Connecticut
- **OneUnited Bank:** Multiple ATM locations[21]

Delaware
- **OneUnited Bank:** Multiple ATM locations[21]

District of Columbia
- **Industrial Bank:** District of Columbia (Anacostia Gateway Banking Center, Ben's Chili Bowl, DC Court of Appeals, DC Superior Court, F Street Banking Center, Forestville Banking Center, Georgia Avenue Banking Center, J.H. Mitchell Banking Center, Nationals Park, Oxon Hill Banking Center, U Street Banking Center[29]
- **Howard University Employees Federal Credit Union:** C B Powell Building[30]

Florida
- **OneUnited Bank:** Multiple ATM locations, in addition to the Miami Branch[21]
- **FAMU Federal Credit Union:** Tallahassee[31]

Georgia
- **OneUnited Bank:** Multiple ATM locations[21]
- **Carver State Bank:** Savannah[32]
- **Citizens Trust Bank:** Atlanta, Decatur, East

Point, Lithonia, Stone Mountain, Stonecrest[23]
- **Unity National Bank:** Atlanta[33]
- **1st Choice Credit Union:** Atlanta[34]
- **Credit Union of Atlanta:** Atlanta[35]
- **Omega Psi Phi Fraternity Federal Credit Union:** Toccoa[36]

Hawaii
- **OneUnited Bank:** Multiple ATM locations[21]

Idaho
- **OneUnited Bank:** Multiple ATM locations[21]

Illinois
- **OneUnited Bank:** Multiple ATM locations[21]
- **GN Bank:** Chicago[37]
- **Liberty Bank:** Forest Park[38]
- **South Side Community Federal Credit Union:** Chicago[39]

Indiana
- **OneUnited Bank:** Multiple ATM locations[21]

Iowa
- **OneUnited Bank:** Multiple ATM locations[21]
- **First Security Bank:** Aredale, Charles City, Dumont, Hampton, Ionia, Manly, Marble Rock, Nora Springs, Riceville, Rockford, Rockwell, Rudd, and Thornton[40]

Kansas
- **OneUnited Bank:** Multiple ATM locations[21]
- **Liberty Bank:** Kansas City[41]

Kentucky
- **OneUnited Bank:** Multiple ATM locations[21]
- **Liberty Bank:** Louisville[42]

Louisiana
- **OneUnited Bank:** Multiple ATM locations[21]
- **Liberty Bank:** Baton Rouge and New Orleans[43][44]
- **Hope Credit Union:** New Orleans[27]
- **Southern Teachers & Parents Federal Credit Union:** Baton Rouge and Thibodaux[45]

Maine
- **OneUnited Bank:** Multiple ATM locations[21]

Maryland
- **OneUnited Bank:** Multiple ATM locations[21]
- **The Harbor Bank of Maryland:** Baltimore, Randallstown, and Silver Spring[46]

Massachusetts
- **OneUnited Bank:** Multiple ATM locations, in addition to the Corporate Headquarters and the Roxbury Branch[21]

Michigan
- **OneUnited Bank:** Multiple ATM locations[21]
- **First Independence Bank:** Clinton Township and Detroit[47]
- **Liberty Bank:** Detroit[48]

Minnesota
- **OneUnited Bank:** Multiple ATM locations[21]

Mississippi
- **OneUnited Bank:** Multiple ATM locations[21]
- **Liberty Bank:** Jackson[49]
- **Hope Credit Union:** Biloxi, Drew, Greenville, Jackson, Louisville, Macon, Moorhead, Robinsonville, Shaw, Terry, Utica, and West Point[27]

Missouri
- **OneUnited Bank:** Multiple ATM locations[21]
- **Liberty Bank:** Kansas City[50]
- **St. Louis Community Credit Union:** Ferguson, Florissant, Pagedale, Richmond Heights, St. John, St. Louis, University City, and Wellston[51]

Montana
- **OneUnited Bank:** Multiple ATM locations[21]

Nebraska
- **OneUnited Bank:** Multiple ATM locations[21]

Nevada
- **OneUnited Bank:** Multiple ATM locations[21]

New Hampshire
- **OneUnited Bank:** Multiple ATM locations[21]

New Jersey
- **OneUnited Bank:** Multiple ATM locations[21]
- **Industrial Bank:** Newark[29]

New Mexico
- **OneUnited Bank:** Multiple ATM locations[21]

New York
- **OneUnited Bank:** Multiple ATM locations[21]
- **Carver Federal Savings Bank:** Brooklyn, Jamaica, and New York City[52]
- **Industrial Bank:** New York City[53]
- **Urban Upbound Federal Credit Union:** Long Island City[54]

North Carolina
- **OneUnited Bank:** Multiple ATM locations[21]
- **Mechanics & Farmers Bank:** Charlotte, Durham, Greensboro, Raleigh, and Winston-Salem[55]
- **First Legacy Community Credit Union:** Charlotte[56]
- **Greater Kinston Credit Union:** Kinston[57]

North Dakota
- **OneUnited Bank:** Multiple ATM locations[21]

Ohio
- **OneUnited Bank:** Multiple ATM locations[21]
- **Faith Community United Credit Union:** Cleveland[58]
- **Toledo Urban Federal Credit Union:** Toledo[59]

Oklahoma
- **OneUnited Bank:** Multiple ATM locations[21]

Oregon
- **OneUnited Bank:** Multiple ATM locations[21]

Pennsylvania
- **OneUnited Bank:** Multiple ATM locations[21]
- **United Bank of Philadelphia:** Philadelphia[60]
- **Hill District Federal Credit Union:** Pittsburgh[61]

Rhode Island
- **OneUnited Bank:** Multiple ATM locations[21]

South Carolina
- **OneUnited Bank:** Multiple ATM locations[21]
- **OPTUS Bank:** Columbia[62]
- **Brookland Federal Credit Union:** West Columbia[63]
- **Community Owned Federal Credit Union:** Charleston[64]

South Dakota
- **OneUnited Bank:** Multiple ATM locations[21]

Tennessee
- **OneUnited Bank:** Multiple ATM locations[21]
- **Citizens Bank:** Memphis and Nashville[65]
- **Tri-State Bank:** Memphis[66]
- **Hope Credit Union:** Jackson and Memphis[27]

Texas
- **OneUnited Bank:** Multiple ATM locations[21]
- **Unity National Bank:** Houston and Missouri City[33]
- **Faith Cooperative Credit Union:** Dallas[67]
- **Mount Olive Baptist Church Federal Credit Union:** Dallas[68]

- **Oak Cliff Christian Federal Credit Union:** Dallas[69]

Utah
- **OneUnited Bank:** Multiple ATM locations[21]

Vermont
- **OneUnited Bank:** Multiple ATM locations[21]

Virginia
- **OneUnited Bank:** Multiple ATM locations[21]
- **Virginia State University Federal Credit Union:** South Chesterfield[70]

Washington
- **OneUnited Bank:** Multiple ATM locations[21]

West Virginia
- **OneUnited Bank:** Multiple ATM locations[21]

Wisconsin
- **OneUnited Bank:** Multiple ATM locations[21]
- **Columbia Savings & Loan:** Milwaukee[71]

Wyoming
- **OneUnited Bank:** Multiple ATM locations[21]

My brothers and sisters, again I cannot stress enough how important it is to put our hard-earned money in black based financial institutions, such as the black banks or the black credit unions listed on the previous pages. These institutions are supposed to be the backbone of our community, yet so many times they are not. Studies show that there are approximately 41 black owned banks and credit unions totaling approximately 6.7 billion dollars in assets. That's only about half of 1% of our 1.2 trillion dollars in spending power, a spending power that has gone up since I've written this book. Think about that, less than half of 1% of our wealth is in our own banks and credit unions.

Unfortunately, we've fallen victim to the "all lives matter", integration propaganda pushed by our beloved ancestor Dr. Martin Luther King Jr. If we are going to speak truthfully, he is the reason why a lot of us are in the position we're in economically, based on the message he pushed on the importance of integration. In an economical sense we start believing as black people that white financial institutions are the best place for our money rather than our own. However, by stating this I am in no way trying to disrespect our beloved ancestor, he was doing what he thought was best for his people at the time. Yet, history has shown us that integration was a mistake, a mistake that even Dr. King realized towards the end of his life, due to the fact that he knew the struggle for integration would ultimately become a struggle for economic rights, in which Dr. King told Harry Belafonte before his death *"I've come upon something that disturbs me deeply, we have fought hard and long for integration, I believe we should have and I know that we will win. I have come to believe I have integrated my people into a burning house".*

This is a statement that he later followed with a

call for Action on April 3rd, 1968 in his final speech *I've been to the Mountain Top* in Memphis, where Dr. King said, "*we've got to strengthen black intuitions. I call upon you to take your money out of the banks downtown* (meaning the white Banks) *and deposit your money in tri–State Bank* (A black bank). *We want a banking movement in Memphis*". However, unfortunately these things are never spoken about in our school systems, public or private, nor will it ever be, while living under a system of white supremacy. As a result of King's call for action not being heard by the masses of our people, black owned banks have been on a steady decline since he made the speech in 1968.

According to the *Huffington Post,* dozens of black owned banks have either closed or been sold since the 1990s. There are currently 19 banks that are primarily black owned in America. Yet the most important stat to remember though, is unlike most major banks, individually no black bank has yet to obtain a billion dollars in assets. Compare that to the East West Bank that we discussed earlier that catered to the Asian community, which in return sits on upwards of 50 billion dollars in total assets. Now how much of that do you think they're giving out to our brothers and sisters in Los Angeles, Atlanta, or New York? We give our money to people outside the black community and what do they give us in return? I will tell you, fewer loans, higher interest rates, redlining and a heavy dose of other discriminatory mortgage lending practices.

For example, in January of 2017, the department of Justice sued Klein Bank for engaging in redlining against what they say were minorities in the community. In the lawsuit, the federal government alleges that from 2010 to at least 2015, Klein Bank structured its home mortgage lending business to serve neighborhoods where the majority of residents are racial and ethnic minorities. Yet the same money they were getting from the minority communities would be used to redline it, helping Klein Bank to acquire over 1.9 billion dollars in total assets, more money than any black owned bank in the country. Now what do these Banks do when they finally decide to give members of our community loans? They jack up the interest rates on them.

Again, in January 2017, (notice I didn't say 1917 because some of us still believe racism is in the past) JP Morgan Chase reached a 53-million-dollar settlement for lending discrimination. Between 2006 and 2009, the Department of Justice discovered that JP Morgan Chase were responsible for approximately 360,000 mortgages. Out of all of those reported loans, 40,000 wholesale loans were made to black borrowers and approximately 66,000 wholesale loans were made to Hispanic borrowers.. But of those 106,000 loans, an estimated 50,000 Black and Hispanic borrowers paid higher rates and fees then similarly situated white borrowers. Therefore, just like Klein Bank, JP Morgan took the black dollar and gave nothing in return.

Our black dollar has helped JP Morgan reach over 2.5 trillion dollars in total assets. That's 500 times the amount of assets in all the black banks put together. As a reminder, these are not isolated incidents, this has been going on for decades, banks holding people in the black community hostage. But now it is time for us to hold them hostage with our 1.2 trillion dollars of annual spending power. Now, I can see some of your faces with a sort of indecisive look. You're saying to yourself "*this sounds good, but you know how black people are with money*". You're asking questions like "*if I put my money in a black bank and they close; I could lose all my money*". Another question you might be pondering about is "*How do I know the black banks won't rip us off as well, or all the nickel and dime fees and headaches I'm going to have because I'm not at a big bank?*". I'm not mad at you for asking those questions, they're good questions. You should always question where you put your money.

So, let me start with this before I answer those questions. I believe that most of our fears and questions we have about banking black come from a deeper place. Let's keep it real for some of you. I can show you the best black bank in the world run by brothers and sisters with PhDs and an excellent track record of empowering the black community yet, for some of you, that still wouldn't be enough. Why is that? The reason is the psychological trauma we are still suffering from slavery. Most of us still believe that any black institution of finance has to be a scheme and cannot be trusted.

Understand we've been so stripped of our

knowledge of self that somehow; we still believe white folks know what's best for us, especially when it comes to money. This is what I mean by mentally enslaved, because just like in slavery, whenever we as black folks would earn a little something on the side we had to give it to white folks. Nothing has changed today. When we make a couple of million, who do we give it to?, white folks. You see, we must begin to reset our minds.

That's why in my 3 keys to empowerment, knowledge of self is before economics, because when you gain knowledge of self you learn to trust your fellow black brother or sister with your personal needs. You also realize that you can prosper financially without the overseeing of white folks. I understand that you may have been with a black bank before and they were slow and maybe even a little unprofessional, but we have to show patience in order to prosper financially. Do you think banks like East-West started off with the best service? Yet the Chinese community supported them. They knew it was bigger than service, it was about economic empowerment, that the bank could one day provide in the future.

So, before you walk into a black bank you need to go in with a fresh mind and knowledge of oneself. Yet with that being said, to answer some of the technical questions you might have like "*could I lose my money if the banks closed*"? That answer is simple. Every bank that I have provided to you is a FDIC approved member including One-United the online-based black Bank. Why is this important? Because all FDIC member banks are insured up to $250,000 per depositor, which means in the case of the bank closing, your account is hacked, or fraud is committed, up to $250,000 in your account will be replaced. This is the exact same amount that other big banks such as Bank of America or Chase, guarantee.

Same thing goes if you decide to choose a black Credit Union. All the credit unions that I have provided are insured by the NCUA. The NCUA just like the FDIC insures your capital up to $250,000. Again, that's the same amount of security you're going to receive at a white owned credit Union. Now that we have solved that issue, let's move on to the next question that might be flooding your mind. That is *"if I do take my money and put it in a black Bank how do I know they won't do the same thing that the white Banks do? Such as redlining, charging higher loan rates, or just flat out not giving me loans?"*

Well according to the FDIC, who is the very people who insure your money, in their minority repository institution research study from 2001 to 2013, statistics showed that minority depository institutions are significantly more likely to lend in low-to-moderate income communities and to minority borrowers, than non-low to moderate-income communities. The FDIC study also showed that African American minority depository institutions appear to be particularly successful in their mission of serving the black community. For example, one study by the FDIC shows that of Home Loans made to black borrowers in 2011,

67% were from black banks, compared to less than 1% from other community banks in that year. Proof that banking black has its perks and rewards when the community is behind it. Last but not least, you might be asking about fees and additional charges because you're not with one of the big Banks.

Yes, it is true that if you bank black you are probably going to pay some of the additional ATM fees, or it might take you a little longer to get your money out. These are things I cannot argue with. However, I will say this, would you rather pay an additional two or three dollars in ATM fees banking black, or have your home loan denied banking white? Would you rather pay a little extra money in transaction fees banking black, or a 40% interest rate on your business loan banking white? Would you rather wait a little bit longer to get your money out banking black, or never see the fruits of depositing that money banking white? Thus, the decision is on you.

If you believe saving a couple hundred dollars in fees is equivalent to the amount you're going to pay back on a loan from a white Bank, go for it, more power to you. If you are using your head however, you know what the correct answer to the question is, bank black. I'll end with this. Banks and credit unions from other communities most times will allow you to get a car loan or student loan. Yet in most cases, they will not give you a housing loan and especially not a business loan because our oppressor is never going to finance our empowerment.

Investing the Black Dollar

By now, every black person in America knows or has heard about the huge wealth gap between white families and black families. We touched on it a little bit in the last section, banking black, but to paint a clearer picture of the situation listen to this. In a 2017 study by Yale University, statistics showed that black families in America earn $57.30 for every $100 a white family earns. Also, for every $100 in wealth accumulated by an average white family, the black family holds $5.40. Mr. Michael Kraus, the psychologist who conducted the research for the study was even shocked at the magnitude in the black-white wealth gap. As well as the amount of equality that still exists in today's economic landscape.

Now, I for one, do agree that a lot of the spread in the black, white wealth gap comes from hundreds of years of systematic economic racism. One could simply write a whole book on the tactics and strategies placed on African people by the government and white supremacists to keep us from acquiring wealth through real estate, and other assets. This is an argument that we could win easily. However, we know that living in a system of white supremacy in America or all the world for that matter, it will take a long time for us to finally receive proper reparations or compensation for our 500 plus year Holocaust that we are still continuing to suffer from. Now I am not giving up on reparations and I know that we will get what's owed to us in full, but in due time.

So, the question then becomes 'what do we do to improve our economic situation in America right now'? Speaking from a family point of view, when we talk banking black, that is supposed to be the rock of the community. The key word being the community, not family. The purpose of banking black is not for everyone to become wealthy. The purpose of banking black is for our community to have access to wealth. We must understand the difference.

You can ask any of our brilliant financial minds a Dr. Boyce Watkins, Suzanne Shank, or a Dr. Claude Anderson and more. No one becomes wealthy by just saving. Saving creates comfort not wealth. Not to say that saving is not important, but it is not meant to grow over time, just meant to act as a safety net. I say that to say this, part of the reason why the wealth gap between black and white people is so big, is because of stock market participation. Yes, that's right stock market participation, white households typically have 3 times the amount of money invested in the stock market, than non-white families have. The word stock market in itself is more like a forbidden word in the black community.

I remember the first time I told my mother I had invested $200 in the stock market, my sophomore year in college. I still to this day remember her reaction, she looked at me out of the corner of her eye and said, "*boy don't start gambling with your money*". I still joke with her about that to this day. That stuck with me for a long time, and I found it to be the common answer when I try to get black people to invest. However, I was never mad at them for not investing or questioning why to invest, because I knew it was part of the culture, we had been brought up in. A culture of white supremacy that instilled in us that the only way for a young black man or woman to gain wealth in this country was through three choices.

First choice was to engage in illegal activities and help to tear down the community. The second choice was to be an Entertainer of some form, whether sports or music. Finally, the third choice is to go to college and get a degree and hopefully one day someone would give you a six-figure job. Coming out of high school I had this mentality and decided to take path number two. I was stuck in that mindset for a long time, until I got hurt in my freshman year of college playing football. To this day I still say that was the best thing that ever happened to me. It allowed me to get off the physical and get on the mental.

So, I understand what it's like to be in that sunken place to believe you're only as valuable as the skills you possess physically. In fact, if someone were trying to tell me about investing my money in the stock market about 6 or 7 years before I wrote this book, I too would have given them the same look my mom gave me. But now that I have woken up and become conscious of oneself and surroundings, I'm here to tell you there's another way, the smart way, the power way, and the need way.

So, moving forward in this section I want to convince you why you must invest in the stock market. I ask that you please listen and keep an open mind and as always don't take it from me do the research yourself. As it's my goal that by the end of this section you will be able to make your first small investment into the market or at least be more comfortable about how it works.

We will discuss six key points in order to convince you of why you should invest in the stock market. We will discuss what stocks are, breaking down exactly what you are buying with your money. Secondly, we will discuss the history of the stock market and its return over the last hundred plus years. Next, we will discuss some of the options of the stocks you can pick to start investing. Fourth we will discuss what mutual funds are and ETF's and what the differences are and the benefits of the two. Then after that we will discuss how to bet against the market, and ways we can even make money as the market is moving down. Last but not least, we will discuss the stock market's performance compared to the bank, comparing the two sides to see which one gives you the better results.

First let's start with the simple question what are stocks? A stock or equity as it is sometimes called, is a security that signifies ownership in a corporation and represents a claim on part of the corporation's assets and earnings. This allows a normal everyday working-class person who may be of low income, to take $100 or less for example, and invest it into a well-known company such as Starbucks, Twitter, or Nike, in return for part ownership of that company. Now one of the more common questions or should I say fears about stocks, are their liquidity. Liquidity meaning the degree in which the stock can be quickly sold in the market for cash. This is a good question for new investors. Stocks are considered to be financial assets, meaning they are paper assets that can be turned into cash rather easily.

Now, small stocks that are known in the stock market world as penny stocks, may be in some cases a little less liquid. I would not advise you to start with penny stocks because they require more skill and experience to trade. However, your big-time companies I want you to start making your investments in are highly liquid. Companies such as Google, Apple, Amazon and more, Fortune 500 companies that are offered on the stock market, trade hundreds of millions of shares a day. Therefore, they can turn your cash into stock or your stock into cash in fractions of a second.

One thing you should know on the backside of that is once your stock is sold it usually takes a minimum three days to settle before you can take it out. However, you will still receive the same money you sold the stock for, but by formality it would take 3 days before you can remove it from your account. Moving forward there are three great things about stocks that I personally love, and I think you will too once you start to invest in the market. First being that stocks just like land, have the ability to appreciate over time. There is no set limit on how much your stock can be worth as well there is no time restriction on the amount of time you can hold it. If you wanted to buy some shares of stock and hold it to pass on to your kids, you could do so.

No one can buy or sell that stock for you, because you are the owner, which leads me to the second thing that is great about stocks. You are allowed to be part owner in the company without any headaches of being an owner. You don't have to keep up with the profits or revenue. You don't have to deal with any employee drama. You just kick back and let someone else handle that.

Yet if you do worry about that type of stuff, as stockholders like yourself, you have the right to vote on certain corporate matters. Shareholders typically have the rights to vote in elections for the board of directors, proposed corporate changes, and shifts of corporate aims and goals of fundamental structural changes. Shareholders like yourself also have the right to vote on matters that directly affect their stock ownership, such as the company doing a stock split or proposed merger or acquisition. You may also have the right to vote on executive compensation packages and administrative issues. Again, all the while not having to do the real work and management of an owner.

Last but not least, some stocks have the ability of producing dividends. Once you begin to make your first investment into the market, the word dividend is going to be your new favorite word to hear. So, what are these dividends and what can it do for you? Well, the technical definition for dividend is a distribution of a portion of a company's earnings decided by the board of directors, to a class of its shareholders. In other words, the company you have partial ownership in, is paying or rewarding you just for being an owner. Dividend stocks are what many billionaires and Wall Street experts consider to be recession-proof.

These companies usually produced reasonable payouts to their shareholders year after year. Many of these are known as Blue Chip stocks meaning the best of the best. Thus, they are known to produce whether it's a recession or not. These are some great stocks to own if you are just looking to invest in dividend stocks. All in all, dividends are just one of the many features of stocks that you will learn to love.

Now that you know what stocks are and some of the benefits that come with them, let's discuss the history of stocks, in order to see for yourself what we individually, as well as a community have been missing out on. A common myth that has fled our community for years has been that if you put your money into the stock market, you're going to lose it all. This is a myth that we must put to rest once and for all in our community. Let's start by looking at the rate of return the stock market has produced over the last 100 years going all the way back to 1917 on the Dow Jones historical chart. For those of you wondering what the Dow Jones is or what its significance is, let me tell you.

The Dow Jones Industrial Average or DJIA for short, is the price weighted average of 30 significant stocks traded on the New York Stock Exchange and the NASDAQ. The Dow is one of the oldest and most watched indices in the world. With companies such as Apple, American Express, Goldman Sachs, IBM, Walt Disney, and more big-name companies making it up. The Dow represents 30 of the most highly capitalized and influential companies in the US economy. The Dow is also the financial media's most referenced U.S market index and a rather good indicator of the general market trends. In return, history has shown us that as the Dow goes, the rest of the market goes. Take a look at the Dow over the last 100 years.

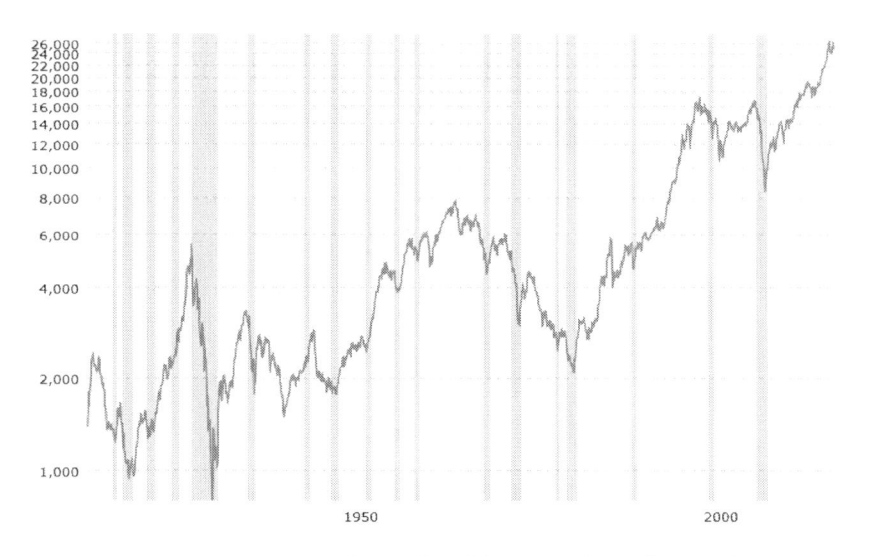

As you can see from looking at the chart, the Dow has been very kind to its long-term investors over the last 100 years. From the year 1917 when the Dow was at about 1852 points, more than a hundred years after that, at the beginning 2017 it set at 19,864. Also, as I write this book today January 29th, 2021, the Dow currently sits at 29,982 points. This is an amazing amount of wealth that was created over the last century until now. Let me give you an example.

If your great great grandfather or grandmother had taken $1,000 and invested it into the stock market in the year 1900, it would have been worth 19.8 million dollars by the end of the century. That's a 19,800 % return rate on your money. We are talking about generational wealth being created over the decades. What makes it even more amazing is that the 20th century was a rough century economically, and politically speaking for the United States. During the twentieth century we saw two world wars, the Great Depression, over a dozen recessions, a presidential assassination, not to mention several cases of social unrest like the Civil Rights Movement. Yet the Dow still produced a 19,800 % return for investors willing to take the chance, a chance that history has shown us to be worth it.

Let's take the time to focus on one of those key events, being the Great Depression. Now if you probably turn on the TV right now and turn to any financial channel such as Bloomberg or Fox Business, you will probably hear the word depression once every hour. Then, you'll probably hear a financial analyst mention that the next Great Depression is around the corner. That you should not invest your money because the hammer is about to come down on the stock market and that this time it will take another 50 years for the market to recover. Now before you get ready to fall out of your chair, take a deep breath. Let's look at the facts, because surveys show that one of the biggest concerns of new investors in the stock market is the fear of another Great Depression and losing their hard-earned money.

When we look at the Great Depression it was the deepest economic downturn of the Western industrialized world. From 1929 to 1939 during the Depression, we saw the worst return on the stock market in its long history. However, with that being said, the facts are this, if you had invested during the height of the stock market in1929, you only saw a loss of about 0.63% on your investment a decade later. So, for example, if great grandfather had invested $1,000 at the height the market in 1929, a decade later, after the full blow of the Great Depression, he would have only lost $6.30. Not bad right, for the greatest economic collapse in the United States history.

Notice that this is the worst return ever decade to decade. Therefore, the key thing I want you to take away from the Great Depression is to hold for the long term. Something that can be very tough for us in today's time. We live in an age where everything is right now. Especially in the black community where we are in love with instant gratification. If I go right now and tell one of our brothers and sisters to start investing so they can have some extra money for retirement, most would look at me like I'm crazy, because we are in the get money and blow it fast and do it all over again era.

Now don't get me wrong, nothing is wrong with "right now money" or "new money". You need your day-to-day money to take care of your everyday living expenses and other needs. However, the problem comes in when you just focus all of your attention on the new money and not give it a chance to mature. You see the "*Right now money*" you're chasing is going to get spent right now. Why is that important to know? Because it causes you to keep repeating the same steps. Get money, spend it, repeat, get money, spend it, repeat.

This is what I like to call financial enslavement, because it causes you to be held hostage to the same system that is giving you the money. I'm going to tell you one of the biggest secrets that every billionaire or millionaire knows about money. Are you ready? "*Money isn't s***!*" Yes, that is correct money isn't s***! What you can do with your money and what it can buy is the real power of money.

However, money in itself is nothing. Let me explain, let's say you work 2 weeks straight at Walmart pushing carts for 8 hours a day, which is in most cases a typical job for a lot of college students, your reward at the end of those two weeks is 500 maybe $600 depending on the number of hours you worked. Now you just worked two weeks of corporate slavery for a check. The first thing we do is pay the bills we have to take care of, then like most of us we celebrate in some form or fashion, buying shoes, clothes, drinking and clubbing, only to realize that 2 days later, that check you received from those two weeks of corporate slavery is gone. 80 hours of slave labor for what, a night or two of fun, and some materialistic items?

So, in response what do we do as black people? The same job that we claim to hate because we are held hostage to that new money system, we keep seeking to reacquire the new money to keep up with our current lifestyle. However, this new money system, is different within other communities. Other communities operate using a powernomics system, understanding the process of how money works. We as black people still do not understand this cycle so in return, we have not attempted to break it. The real power of money is to take it and buy a money machine.

In other words, making your money work for you. Your money always needs to be producing more money. You can't do this with new money because you haven't given it time to mature or reproduce, due to the fact that you just go out and spend it. We have to begin to let our money mature in our money machines. This is what forms of financial assets such as the stock market allow you to create. Therefore, I encourage you to invest in long-term stocks, stocks you plan on holding on to 10 plus years. I say that because when you continue to put your money in the money machine meaning the stock market, you might start out only producing $0.25 a day. To a majority of us that is nothing.

However, as you give it time to mature, two years later it's producing $5 a day. Then five years later is producing $25 a day. Then finally 10 years later $100 a day. All of this can be possible because of the power of compound interest. Compound interest is the addition of interest to the principal sum of a loan or deposit, or in other words interest on top of interest. It comes as a result of the interest you have already gained, rather than taking it out.

Now that interest you left in; next period is then earned on the principal sum plus previously accumulated interest. This explains how your great-great-grandfather could have taken $1,000 and invested into the stock market in 1900, and at the end of the century had 19.8 million without adding anything throughout the years. The famous physicist Albert Einstein said this about compound interest. Compound interest is the eighth wonder of the world. "*He who understands it, earns it...he who doesn't ...pays it*". Long-term investing is the best way to transform our community overnight which will efficiently help us pass money down from generation to generation. Don't be fearful of a stock market crash.

In fact, embrace the next crash if or when it comes. History has shown us the stock market has rewarded the investors who weather the storm. A crash would be the perfect opportunity to swoop up some shares at a huge discount. Anticipation is the ultimate power. Losers react leaders anticipate. So, when everyone is dumping their shares for cheap during a crash, we as members of the black community need to be looking to buy them up, anticipating a bounce back. Be the shark not the school of fish.

Hopefully by now, I have at least sparked your interest into investing in the stock market. If so, the next step is for you. One of the more common questions for new investors finally ready to invest in stocks is, what stocks do I pick? Well before I answer that question, I must explain to you how to buy stocks to begin with. Before you can buy shares of a company, you are going to need a brokerage account. A brokerage account is an arrangement between an investor like yourself and a licensed brokerage firm that allows you to deposit funds with the firm and place investment orders through the Broker. There are plenty of brokerage firms to choose from, Charles Schwab, TD Ameritrade, e-Trade, Merrill Edge, Scottrade and more. I personally use several brokerage accounts all for different purposes.

It's all about finding which one fits you best. Most, if not all of them, are pretty simple to sign up for and create an account. Just make sure whatever company you choose fits you personally. Some brokerage accounts are more technical and advanced, others are simpler and straight to the point. Some may only charge $5 commission on your trades in and out of stock, others may be a little more. Again, it's all about choosing the right one for you. Now back to the initial question of what stocks do I pick? My answer to that question is a lot.

Now I don't mean that in a literal sense. What I mean is a key to having a solid stock portfolio that delivers good interest annually and in the future years is diversification. It's not about what particular stock to pick that will give you that home run return, it's about choosing a multitude of good fundamental and technical stocks. There is a great book by Burton Malkiel, a professor of economics at Princeton University. The book is called "*A Random walk down Wall Street*" it is a must-read for all new investors, because it seems like so many times, we make investing in the stock market rocket science.

In the book "*A Random walk down Wall Street*" Burton Malkiel argues and proves that future stock market prices cannot be predicted based on past market prices and trends. In the book, to prove his theory, Malkiel famously has blindfolded monkeys throw darts at random companies in a newspaper, then he compares the stocks the monkeys picked to expert picks on Wall Street. Guess who won? The monkeys, and by a long shot as well, proving that even a monkey can be a successful stock market investor. But how though? That's probably a question many of you are asking yourself right now. Were these some type of super intelligent monkeys from the future?

The answer is no, but how they did it was simple. One of the biggest reasons the monkeys were so successful was diversification. The monkey didn't care about what company had the best PE Ratio or who had the best earnings. They were just throwing the darts at random companies on the paper, creating a diversified portfolio. What the monkeys showed us is when you diversify your portfolio, you reduce your chances of taking a major loss in the market because you are not just depending on any one stock to make or break you. Diversifying your portfolio is the key to success in the stock market.

Just ask some of these Wall Street billionaires. At the time of me writing this, Warren Buffett owns stocks in over 45 different companies, from Apple to General Motors. George Soros owns stock in over 50 different companies, from Kroger's to Facebook. Carl Icahn owns stock in about 19 different companies, from Chesapeake Energy to Hertz. David Tepper owns stock in about 54 different companies, from Allstate to JC Penney's. Might I add, these are just a few billionaire investors who have a diversified portfolio. That's why there are two points I want to continue to emphasize about your stock market investments.

Number one, diversify your portfolio and number two, hold your investment for the long term to create compound interest. Always keep these two things in mind when investing in the stock market. Yet, I understand that it is easier to say it, than to do it, especially when we are talking in terms of diversifying our portfolio. What I mean by that is diversification costs money, especially when we are talking about investing in the big boy companies of Wall Street. Companies like Amazon, who at the time of me writing this book are going for over $3,200 a share. Facebook is another well-known company going for over $258 a share. Even companies like Google are going for about $1,800 a share.

Now if you try to buy 5 shares of each of these stocks it's going to cost you roughly $20,000. Keeping it real, a lot of us aren't sitting around with $20,000 of investment money to add to our stock market portfolio, and even if we did many are not ready to put that much in the market as a first-time investor. These are all concerns that are completely understandable. That's why I have some solutions for you. The first being mutual funds.

A mutual fund is an investment vehicle made up of a pool of funds collected from many investors for the purpose of investing in securities such as stocks or even bonds, money markets and other similar assets. Now what makes mutual funds great, is they are a cheaper way to create a diversified portfolio of stocks. Most of them start at around $2,500, much cheaper than it would be to create a diversified portfolio on your own. This is probably a great option for those of you who don't want anything to do with the market's up and down swings. Some of us might just want to hand our money to someone and have them invest and take care of it. If that sounds like you, mutual funds are for you.

Mutual funds are diversified and managed by professionals. Adjusting your portfolio to the market to get the best performance or return rate possible. Mutual funds also give you a wide range of options to choose from. Brokerage companies such as Fidelity, offer thousands of different mutual funds to choose from, ranging anywhere from international funds dealing with companies overseas, to Marijuana based mutual funds dealing with the legalization of cannabis that is beginning to emerge. With all these options, some mutual funds that you might want to look into diversifying in would be Medical or Health Care funds.

For example, Vanguard Healthcare fund or Price Health Sciences funds are good mutual funds, just to name a couple in the medical field. One thing we know is that everyone is going to get sick and unfortunately die one day. There is always going to be a big need for healthcare and healthcare research in order to cure diseases that affect ourselves and our loved ones every day. Diseases such as cancer, AIDS, Ebola or even Corona Virus. In return, healthcare is always a good sector to invest in, both morally and financially.

The second type of mutual fund you might want to look into investing in, is an energy-based mutual fund. As Dr. Kaba Kamene reminds us all the time, the future of the world is in solar power. Our ancestors understood that a long time ago as the pyramids were indeed power plants. Every country around the world is always looking for alternative forms of energy, due to the depleting natural resources in places around the world. This is one of the main reasons as we discussed before, why other foreign nations are fighting over Africa in countries like Nigeria and Ghana.

We as black people need to start investing in some

of these energy-based funds. Some popular ones are the Vanguard energy fund, which contains companies that conduct oil explorations, production or transmission of energy or fuel, as well as some that just conduct energy research. The last one I'll bring to your attention about possibly investing in is technology based mutual funds. This really needs no explaining on the reason why. Do we do anything today without technology?

Whether it is Face Timing on our iPhone or uploading a story to Snapchat. Technology is a sector that is always evolving and growing. Just look at places like Silicon Valley who has produced more millionaires over the last decade or two than anywhere in the United States. Companies that we know today such as Google, Facebook, Amazon, Yahoo, Snapchat and more. All have come out of Silicon Valley and the technology boom, which makes the technology sector always great for investors. Some brokerages that offer good mutual funds are Fidelity select IT services (FBSOX), Red Oak technology Select Fund (ROGSX), T. Rowe Price global technology fund (PRGTX), and Columbia Seligman Global Technology Fund (SHGTX).

These are some mutual funds you might want to look into, as we are all familiar with the companies that are in them. There are many more types, I just wanted to name a few, to get you interested in the possibilities of investing in diversified portfolios such as technology based mutual funds for the long term. All in all, these mutual funds are a cheaper way to diversify your portfolio. However, for many of us this is still too expensive, even at the discount of $2,500 compared to the possible $20,000 it would take to diversify a portfolio on your own. That's understandable as well, which is why I have an even cheaper and better solution for you.

Let me introduce you to my favorite way of investing which is through ETFs. ETF's stands for Exchange-Traded Funds, which is a marketable security that tracks an index, a commodity, bonds, or a basket of assets. In simpler terms an ETF is a bundle of stocks put together and traded under one stock ticker. It is different from a mutual fund in certain ways. One being that unlike mutual funds, ETF's are a much cheaper way to diversify your portfolio. Also unlike mutual funds, an ETF trades like a common stock making it much easier and quicker to take your money out if you need to. Having higher daily liquidity and lower fees than mutual funds, ETF's are a more attractive alternative for investors looking to diversify.

ETF's are ideal for our brothers and sisters who like me, might be just out of college, in college, high school or outright just new investors, seeing that most of you don't have a couple thousand laying around to invest in a mutual fund. Now the best way in my opinion to start investing in these ETFs is through a company called Stash. What makes Stash special is it makes it easy for any new investor to get their feet wet in the market. Suiting with the whole millennial generation, Stash is an investing app on your phone that can be downloaded, whether you have an iPhone or Android. It allows you to take as little as $5 and invest it into any one of their diversified ETFs. ETFs such as "Blue Chips" allows you to take your 5 dollars and get a fraction of a share from a bundle of companies such as Apple, Microsoft, Amazon, Facebook, Johnson & Johnson, Exxon Mobil, Berkshire Hathaway, JP Morgan, and Google.

Remember all for as little as $5. Not to mention all of this is commission free each time you make a trade. Only charging a $1 monthly fee. I should also point out that Stash is not the only app that allows you to do this. There are other apps such as Stock Pile, Robinhood, Acorn and more. However, I use Stash, this is why I spoke about it in detail. Yet as always, it's about what is the best app for you. This is an amazing opportunity that we need to take advantage of, giving everyone of all ages a chance to create long-term wealth.

Now the only downside about ETFs is they are not managed and adjusted by professionals like mutual funds are. However, remember no one knows whether the market will go up or down as the monkeys proved in *"A random walk down Wall Street"*. Therefore, I suggest that everyone reading this book invest in diversified ETFs using Stash for a cheaper more cost-efficient way of investing. Whether you are rich or poor it is a great way to get your feet wet in the stock market for a low price. Now I know I have some brothers and sisters, who still don't believe in investing in the stock market.

You're watching the news every day seeing all the

rumors swirling around politics and the corona viruses, leading you to believe the stock market will eventually crash down. Even with this state of mind the stock market is still for you. If you are a person who believes the market is going to crash at any time now, guess what? You can bet against the market and make money as well. A common misconception a lot of people have about the market is they think they can only make money when the market is going up. Wrong, you can also make a ton of money when the markets are trending down.

Now before I continue, I would suggest that if you decide to bet against the market you do some further research before starting. However, with practice it can be done. One way is through what are called in the stock market put options. Put options gives investors the right to sell shares of a particular stock or ETF at a price between now and the date in which the option expires. A put option becomes more valuable as the price of the underlying stock or ETF depreciates relative to the strike price. Vice versa a put option becomes less value as the underlying stock increases as the time to expiration approaches.

Let me give you an example as provided to you by Investopedia, which is a great source for any questions you might have pertaining to the stock market. For example, let's say you buy 1 put option on a hypothetical stock called TAZR with a strike price of $25. Strike price meaning where you have the right to sell the stock at. Therefore, you the investor, have the right to sell 100 shares of TAZR at a price of $25 until the expiration date next month. Now let's say shares of TAZR fall to $15 and you exercise your option. You would then purchase 100 shares of TARZ at $15 and then turn around and sell the shares to the options writer for $25 each.

Meaning consequently, you would have made $1,000, because you bought 100 shares at $15 each totaling $1,500, then you turned around and sold those shares for $25 apiece for a total of $2,500, giving you a profit of $1,000. Another more popular form of betting against the stock market is by short-selling. Short Selling is the sale of a stock or ETF that is not owned by the seller who is you, but rather one you have borrowed. If the stock declines as expected, you the short seller will buy it back at a lower price in the market and pocket the difference, which is the profit on the short sale. Short Selling is mainly promoted by speculation or to help hedge some downside risk of a long-term position.

Another example from Investopedia says a stock SS is trading at $50 a share but will decline in price. Therefore, you borrow a hundred shares with the attempt to sell them when the price drops. You have now taken a short position by borrowing shares from the owner, which he may demand back at any point. Now a week later SS stock falls to $45, you decide to close the short position and buy a hundred shares at $5 to replace the borrowed shares. You would then profit on the short sale $500, again, because you borrow the shares $50 each at $45 giving you a chance to pocket the difference of $500.

However, if you do decide to bet against the market by shorting, I want you to be very careful. The reason being that the risk of loss on a short sale is theoretically infinite. Meaning unlike options, there is no time or stop limit. In other words, you could technically run stock SS down to a dollar and have a profit of $4,900 or you could watch it run up to $100 or even higher, forcing you to pay $10,000 for the shares you borrow. That's why I prefer first time traders to stay away from Short Selling until you have some experience under your belt.

All in all, these are some opportunities presented to you as ways of taking advantage of a Down Market. I strongly suggest however, you start off with the simple strategy of buying and holding Diversified ETF's. Moving on to my final persuasive tool in order to get you investing in the market, is by flat out comparing some raw numbers. Numbers between Saving vs. Investing. For those of us who invest in the stock market compared to those who just save their money and put it in the bank.

Let's start with the bank. It does not matter what bank it is black, white, Chinese, etc. The best interest rate you are going to find on your savings account will be no higher than 2.25%. Now let's just say you find this bank and put your hard-earned money in it, with plans to just let it sit and create interest. Using the rule of 72, we know it would take 32 years and eight months to flip your money using the best saving account interest rate.

Now on the flip side let's see what happens if you

were to invest that money into the stock market. We know that give or take a percentage or two the average return on the stock market is roughly 7% annually. That is 5.25% higher than that of the best savings account interest rate. Now again going back to the rule of 72. If you were to invest your money in the stock market and receive just the average rate of return it would only take about 10 years and two months to flip your money. Remember, this is just based on the average annual return in the stock market.

Take for example in 2008 the beginning of the Obama presidency. If we had kept that same energy to invest our money in the stock market while Obama was serving those eight years in the White House, we would have had a return of 235% on our investment based on the Dow Jones index. From Obama's first inauguration on January 20th, 2009, U.S. equities surged an average of 16.4% a year, not counting dividends, in what turned out to be the second longest bull market in history. Bottom line is when you compare the bank versus the stock market as it pertains to gaining generational wealth, the better choice is obvious. Always remember the black bank is still important for the black community, in terms of providing tangible resources to the community. However, the stock market is the key to creating long term generational wealth.

Hopefully in this section I have convinced you to start putting a little of your money to the side, so that you may invest into the stock market in order to create a foundation for the future wealth of yourself and your children. At least this gives you something to think about in the future as it pertains to a place for your money, but I urge you to please not to contemplate this decision for too long. I don't want you to look back 5 or 10 years from now and regret not investing. Understand that the market might seem like a scary place but it's not. We cannot as black people continue to miss out on this incredible money-making opportunity because of fear.

Therefore, if you are sitting up right now reading this book with $250 Jordan's on your feet but no assets to speak of, you need to stop playing yourself. If you find yourself every Super Bowl or finals betting thousands of dollars on the games but have no stocks or assets to speak of, you need to stop playing yourself. If you're walking around with an $800 Gucci belt on, but have no assets to your name, you need to stop playing yourself. It all goes back to how we started the section, talking about guns and butter. Your butter items are materialistic things in life that are going to come and go, and will never reimburse you on your investment. The guns in this case being stocks, will always return your investment and then some. The moral of the story is if you get yourself more guns the butter will naturally come. The real world is chess not checkers. Time to make chess moves.

Buying Black

Earlier in the section while discussing the importance of banking black, we talked about the 1.2 trillion dollars of spending power that we possess. The same spending power we have neglected our black banks with. However, it's not just the black banking institutions we have neglected, it's all black institutions as a whole. Whether it's the black owned nail salon down the street struggling to make ends meet because they can't compete with the low prices of the Chinese nail shop, or the black owned shoe or fashion store that is struggling because customers won't come in as they assume it's ghetto. We are the only race of people who ignore and neglect our own businesses. It's crazy when you think about it.

Take me for example, I was born and raised on the Eastside of Atlanta in a predominantly black neighborhood. I remember I used to have friends who refused to go to the local malls and shops in our community. Instead, they went all the way across town to the north side of Atlanta to go shop at malls like Lenox. A mall that was considered to be on the rich white side of town. Confused as to why they would go way across town to shop there I would question them. Their response would be "it's nicer over there and they have more high-end stuff".

Yet, there was only one problem with their response in my eyes. They would come back with some Air Forces and Nike shirts. These were all items that they could have bought right here from the local black businesses, and malls. I could understand if they came back with more high-end products that we don't have access to in our neighborhoods, but some Nike shoes and shirts "child please". What I realized though was this type of attitude was not just catered to my community. It describes the mentality of a lot of black communities around America.

When we say nicer businesses, we associate that with being whiter businesses. As my grandma used to say, "child some folks just think the white man ice is colder". Proof of this comes in the form of cold hard statistics when comparing the dollar circulation in our community with others. A dollar circulates 30 days in the Asian community before it leaves. The European Jew dollar circulates 20 days in the Jewish community before it leaves. The white dollar circulates 17 days in the white community before it leaves.

Then you get to us, the black dollar circulates just 6 hours before it leaves. Meaning as soon as we get our paycheck, we run to go spend it with members of other communities. This is one of the exact reasons why they laugh at us when we get killed by the police, because they know we're not going to do anything to them physically or economically. It's like we discussed in previous Voice of the Ancestors books, there are only two things white supremacy respects, the loss of life and the loss of finance. As long as you're not affecting those two things, they will continue to oppress us. The 2018 chart below done by the Nielsen company demonstrates the true power of the black dollar and what impact we could have if we retract it.

THE POWER OF BLACK DOLLARS

Categories where the percentage of Black spending is greater
in proportion to their population (14%)

CATEGORY	BLACK SPEND	TOTAL SPEND	% OF TOTAL SPEND ATTRIBUTABLE TO BLACK CONSUMERS
ETHNIC HAIR & BEAUTY AIDS	$54.4M	$63.5M	85.65%
WOMEN'S FRAGRANCES	$152M	$679.4M	22.37%
FEMININE HYGIENE	$54.1M	$257.3M	21.04%
MEN'S TOILETRIES	$62M	$308.3M	20.10%
PERSONAL SOAP & BATH NEEDS	$573.6M	$3.04B	18.89%
FROZEN UNPREPARED MEAT & SEAFOOD	$761.7M	$4.3B	17.75%
REFRIGERATED JUICES & DRINKS	$578.2M	$3.3B	17.51%
SHELF-STABLE JUICES & DRINKS	$1.04B	$6.2B	16.66%
SPICES, SEASONINGS & EXTRACTS	$430.2M	$2.7B	16.13%
BOTTLED WATER	$810.3M	$5.15B	15.74%
INSECTICIDES & REPELLENTS	$176.6M	$1.14B	15.49%
GUM	$122.8M	$807.7M	15.20%
SHORTENING/OIL	$352M	$2.3B	15.05%
HOUSEHOLD CLEANERS	$407.8M	$2.7B	14.89%
DETERGENTS	$829.8M	$5.6B	14.83%
COOKWARE	$136.8M	$934.5M	14.64%
CHARCOAL, LOGS & ACCESSORIES	$43.5M	$300.5M	14.48%

Source: Nielsen Homescan. Total U.S. 52 Weeks ending 12/30/17.

As I mentioned to you in the introduction of this chapter, we are in love with symbolism. Shopping at a black owned business doesn't symbolize success to us, because we see ourselves as charity cases. As if black businesses owe us or something, before we walk in the door. In fact, studies show that black owned businesses only get about 7% to 10% of the black consumer dollar, which is weird, given the fact that after the government, they are the biggest employers of black people. In return, if we spent more of our money with black owned businesses, it would generate nearly 1 million new jobs for black people.

You see this is not about just sending a message to the white man, but all races of people. Now some of you out there might think that's racist, but the facts are we are the only group of people who still believe in a multicultural movement. We are also the only people who attempt to be multicultural when it comes to money. On one hand we will support any group of people. On the other hand, no other group will support us. This is a cycle and a process that we must begin to break, but the real question is how though? because so many times we know the problem but don't know the solution. Of course, the obvious answer is to simply buy black.

However, we all know it can be tough sometimes to find black owned businesses, which leads me to the first step, which is to eliminate the competition, meaning boycott everybody but black businesses in your area. Now if you only have one grocery store for 30 miles, then you have to do what you have to do. However, if there's a black owned soul food restaurant struggling to survive, because he's competing with the two Chinese owned soul food restaurants down the street that is a problem. Those Chinese soul food restaurants should not receive another dollar from us. It's not about racism it's about survival.

We must take the pan-African approach moving forward meaning black first. At the end of the day the only people who are going to take care of the black community are black people. Spending your money with black businesses only creates a sort of protective wall around your community. Look at other communities for example. If I were a successful black businessman trying to open a business in Chinatown, I would be hit with some major obstacles to deter me from doing so.

First one is the Chinese store owners along with other members of the community, people who will do their best to try and prevent me from building a store in their community in the first place. They will go to the local politicians and government officials to prevent me from even receiving building permits to open a business in Chinatown. Then if I were somehow able to escape the first attack, they would move on to the next step which would be boycotting. I would receive little to no business from the Chinese people in that area. They would personally boycott and encourage others to follow suit as well. This would for sure put me out of business.

This happens all the time and is not seen as racism, because it's not. The Chinese simply understand powernomics and the fact that I would never value and honor their dollar like they would. So, in return they wouldn't risk me taking their money and putting it into another community. Everything in Chinatown is for the Chinese. Whether it be banks, food, clothes etc. Everything is catered to them which as I stated before is not the problem.

Yet when we allow them to take over our community that is problem. See, we've allowed the government to pull the wool over our eyes and convince us to let them come in because they're going to build businesses, which will provide jobs to the community and help empower it. This is a completely false statement and narrative. Members of the Chinese community and every other community do the same thing they always do, which is take your money and employ and empower their own people. When is the last time you've seen a Chinese store in the black community, with someone other than an Asian person working them?

Almost never, and when you do see it you damn near have to take a picture of it. That's because the Chinese are going to keep their money in their family and in their community. As their business grows, they are just going to invite over more family from their homeland. You would at least think with all the money they make in the black community that they would at least help to provide a voice to black genocide at the hands of the police. Yet where is the Chinese community in the protest of the killing of unarmed black men, women, and children.

In fact, where are any of these groups that leech off the black community when these killings happen? Where are the East Indian or the Arab communities, who damn near own every gas station in the black community, but when it's time to stand with us over police killings along with other issues, they're nowhere to be found? See, we don't understand when members of other communities come to America from other countries, they are specifically told what businesses to start and where. They are told to set up shop in the black community because they know we have no type of commitment to black businesses. Even when you look at black nations around the world, foreigners come in with the same mentality.

Take Jamaica for example, an island which if the native people are not careful won't be black for long. In fact, some will argue Jamaica is already a Chinese colony now. Most will agree if our brothers and sisters in Jamaica don't stop selling out contracts for business, constructing, and land to China and other foreigners, Jamaica will definitely be a Chinese colony in another decade. I also told you in Voice of the Ancestors VI how throughout Africa, the white man and the Chinese man are fighting over the mother continent. I can go on and on about the black community and countries being taken over by members of other nations.

Therefore, boycotting is an important step to taking back our community. History has shown us that some of the most successful rebellions have happened through economic boycotts. The Montgomery Bus Boycott for example, was one of the most successful and impactful movements during the Civil Rights era. So much so, that to this day the dominant society tries not to bring it up. The Montgomery Bus Boycott was a social and political protest for racial segregation on the public bus system in Montgomery Alabama. As many of us know during that time in America, we were restricted to certain seating areas when it came to public transportation.

In the case of the Montgomery busing system, blacks were forced to sit on the back of the bus, or forced to give up their seat if a white person needed one, no matter what section they were in. These were the laws of the racist Jim Crow South that Rosa Parks challenged on December 1st, 1955, when Ms. Parks refused to obey James F. Blake's order to give up her seat in the colored section to the white passenger. Now it is important to note, that contrary to popular belief she was not the first black woman or man to refuse to give up her seat. People such as Claudette Colvin refused to get up before her. However, nonetheless she became a symbol and icon of the movement because she was college educated and a law-abiding citizen of the working class.

As a result of this, it caused massive protests in Montgomery, when leaders of the black community in Montgomery decided to come together and protest, not by marching though, but boycotting the busing system entirely. This was a bold but very smart decision that was really the first major one of its kind during the Civil Rights era. It's important we understand with the elders understood then, what we seem to forget about in today's time. That is, money speaks louder than words. Our elders knew that at least 75% of the Montgomery's Bus Riders were black. In return if every black person in Montgomery stopped riding the bus, it would have huge economic repercussions.

It started with the women's political Council led by Jo Ann Robinson who printed and circulated flyers throughout the black community, urging the community whether, man, woman, or child, old or young, not to ride the bus on the following Monday morning after Park's arrest. On December 5th, 1955 Dr. Martin Luther King, who wasn't recognized at the time, made the final rallying call for the boycott in which the black community agreed, as a result, from December 5th, 1955 to December 20th, 1956, for 385 days few, if any people from the black community rode the public busing system. Even our elders did whatever it took to stay off the public busing system. Instead of riding buses, boycotters organized a system of carpools, volunteering their vehicles or even themselves to drive to various destinations. When the city pressured the local insurance companies to stop insuring cars used in carpools, leaders from our community arranged policies at local insurance companies.

In support of the boycott, many brothers and sisters who were cab drivers would only charge $0.10 per ride, which was equivalent to the cost of the bus at the time. When the system of white supremacy tried to take that away by fining any cab drivers who charged less than $0.45 it still didn't stop the movement. Many black cab drivers took the fine and even were arrested for not changing their prices. In addition, many of our elders used non-motorized means to get around, such as walking, cycling, or even riding mules or driving horses drawn by buggies. Across the nation, black churches raised the money to support the boycott and collected new and slightly used shoes to replace the tattered footwear of Montgomery's black citizens.

Even when white supremacists used acts of violence to protest, such as the bombing of Dr. Martin Luther King's house, our elders continued their protest in unity. From young to old, from rich to poor, the black community stayed on code. As a result, pressure increased on the city of Montgomery, and the state of Alabama as a whole, from the economic and social unrest. The system of white supremacy in Montgomery was losing money and white folks were losing jobs, especially ones in the transportation system, leading to the United States court decision on November 13th, 1956, to uphold the Federal District Court's decision in Browder vs. Gayle, stating that Alabama's racial segregation laws for buses were unconstitutional. Only then did the boycott officially end and we began riding the busing system.

It wasn't about asking, and it wasn't about begging. It was about hitting the system of white supremacy in their pockets in order to create change. This is an event in our history that we must learn from and apply to our situation going forward. Not only learning from them but improving these methods of economic boycotting. What I mean by that is as great as the Montgomery Bus Boycott was, one thing I wish we could have done, was make and build our own. Taking the money that was raised in the collection plate on Sunday at the church and use it to build our own bus lines, as well as create our own line of black taxis and other forms of public transportation. This is why the black dollar needs to stay in the black community.

We achieved our goals in the Montgomery Bus Boycott in an efficient way, but we also in a way let the system of white supremacy off the hook, because as soon as they let us sit anywhere on the bus, we gave them our money right back, which led again to the empowering of our oppressors. Not to be too critical of the past though, because it's about what we can learn from this moving forward. Although we are not dealing with the same form of racism, as back in the 1950s and 60s, we can still use forms of economic boycotting to create change in the black community. Now how does economic boycotting tie back into buying black? It decreases the competition from outside competitors so black businesses can survive and thrive. Therefore, making it an easier decision for us to buy black because that's the only choice we have.

The only competition to black businesses in a black community should be other black businesses. Again however, this starts with us being able to buy black in our own community. Are we going to stay on code and stick through with the boycott or are we going to continue to give our money to the Chinese, Arabs, Whites, etc.? Start by making a pledge that from your next check, the first dollar you spend out of it will go into another black hand. Then begin to work your way up to 50%, and so on until all your money goes into black owned businesses.

Websites such as "we buy black" or "buy black movement" and more will help you do so in a more efficient way. If we do these things, I promise you the circulation of the black dollar in our community will increase from 6 hours. Not only will the circulation increase but the community will also. There will be more jobs and opportunities for members of our community, but it all starts with us staying on code, making it a priority to buy from your fellow black brother and sister to help create a foundation for our community.

Economic Power of Choice

As I sit here as a young black man in America, I

am sometimes baffled at what I see, because when we talk about the economic power of choice, none of us have a more powerful choice to make than our black kings and queens who are entertainers, athletes or political figures, more so speaking to the athletes, because the pool of black athletes in America are a walking trillion-dollar asset, an asset that can be called one of America's richest natural resources. We are a group of people who have not realized the economic impact we possess as a unit; therefore, we are constantly stuck in the same slave mentality and slave system. We were discussing earlier in the stock market section of this chapter how some of us have become corporate slaves. Becoming attached to the corporate plantation for money. However, that does not just apply to the everyday working class of black people. That same system applies to the richest of us also.

The less than 1% of the black population who most of which are professional athletes. Yet even though most of our black athletes are financially free, they are also enslaved. Meaning in a certain sense, we have some of our black athletes who are enslaved to the corporate plantation financially, yet are free thinkers, vice versa, we have some of our black athletes who have true financial freedom but are enslaved mentally. Now to get a little bit deeper into the concept of what I am talking about, let me give you an example. First, dealing with the situation of athlete number one who has the freedom of mind, yet is a slave to the system financially. Look at today's NFL aka the Negro for lease organization.

Colin Kaepernick Taking a Knee

We all know by now that our brother Colin Kaepernick has awakened the masses of all Americans as it pertains to the situation of police brutality that affects the black community every day. As a result of the situation, our brother Colin Kaepernick has received a backlash from the masses of white America, which is by no surprise, living in a system of white supremacy, in fact it should be expected. The interesting thing though, is how the masses of black people reacted around the country. Particularly our professional black athletes.

Notice that some of our black athletes approached it from the first standpoint I mentioned.

NFL players who have some form of knowledge of self-understood where Colin Kaepernick was coming from and were willing to speak out on the social injustices. Yet on the flip side many did not want to take a knee in an act of unity towards the issue of police brutality. Most of the time this happens because these players are enslaved financially. Therefore, when their white owner is tired of hearing them talk on the issue, they snap their fingers, and the players hop right back in line. This comes from the same bad financial habits our brothers and sisters who work at Walmart possess that I spoke about earlier in the section. Financial enslavement is one way some of our most conscious black athletes are even held in check.

Notice how you hear some of them when asked about protesting the national anthem say something like "I got a family to feed" or "bills to pay". Yet they have earned 60 million dollars plus, in their NFL career already. They're financial slaves no matter how woke they may be. Then you have the second kind of black NFL player, who's financially free but has no knowledge of self. They could retire today and be well off. Their kids, and kid's kids will never have to work for anybody because not only did they make millions of dollars in the league, but they made even smarter business moves with the money outside the league.

These athletes tend to fall under the mindset of

having no knowledge of self at all or that "all lives matter", "why can't we get alone" mindset. Normally the athlete with zero knowledge of self-sounds like what his white owner told him to say. They will say what about "black on black crime" or "I'm not going to disrespect the troops". Even though Colin Kaepernick's protest had zero to do with either one of these topics. He clearly stated that he was taking a knee for the unarmed killing of several black men, women, and children at the hands of the police. Yet these black athletes with no knowledge of self will try to deflect the narrative to something else.

Within the same group you have the "all lives matter" athletes. These are our brothers who never choose a side because they don't want to offend anybody. Saying things "like who am I to say that racism does or does not exist" or they will say yeah "the killings of unarmed black men is wrong but America's not perfect and we need to come together and solve our differences". Does any of these quotes sound familiar? As frustrated as it is to watch, I understand that this is a mentality that has been instilled in our black athletes from the first time they start playing.

This is the million-dollar slave mentality. They don't care how much other people mistreat our people because look at what the white man did for me. Just watch the next NBA, NFL, or MLB draft, watch how many of our black athletes that get drafted get up there and say it's an honor to play in the NFL, NBA, or MLB. Watch how many break down crying, thanking their rich white owners for allowing them to be a part of their team. Our black athletes these days have the mindset that they owe these professional leagues something. When in all actuality they don't.

The NFL, The MLB, The NBA however owe them. I don't think I have ever been to an NFL game and heard someone say I'm here to see Arthur Blank or Jerry Jones. I don't think I've heard any fan of the NBA say they're going to the game to see Dan Gilbert or Joseph Lacob and Peter Guber. Most of you reading this right now are like, "I don't even know who the hell these people are". These are the owners of some of your favorite professional sports teams, the cowboys, falcons, cavilers, and warriors. Yet most of you don't know their names and most Americans don't care to know their names.

The reason being, you don't come to the game to see the owners, you come to the game to see the players, most of whom are black. Yet when our black brothers and sisters try to speak out against inequality, they are told to shut up, look at how much you get paid, it's an honor and a privilege to play in the league. The masses of America especially white, act as if the player's voices and opinions aren't important. Yet the same black players they are calling out are the same reason why they watch the game today. Here's a message to the masses of white America that I want them to understand, and for the millions of black athletes to hear. Just because you pay us doesn't mean you own us.

In fact, the owners of every League should be getting down on their knees catering to the black athlete and thanking them. See, the fans from the outside looking in get it confused. They see players such a Steph Curry signing 200-million-dollar deals and think, 'what they are complaining about'? Forgetting the fact that the players on the Golden State Warriors only get paid roughly 36% of the team's total revenue, which in the 2016 season for the Golden State Warriors was about 305 million dollars. At this pace, by the time Stephen Curry received his 201 million, the franchise would have already received roughly 1.5 billion in revenue.

Same thing with NFL teams like the Dallas Cowboys, who paid their players around 177 million dollars in contracts in 2017. Yet in return received 305 million dollars in revenue from ticket sales, concessions, jersey sales, TV contracts and more. By the time their highest-paid player Dez Bryant who was on the team, at the time finished out his 5 years 70-million-dollar deal at the end of 2019 season, the Dallas Cowboys would have made over 2 billion dollars in revenue. Again, why are the owners of these sports teams making so much money? Mostly because of the labor they are exploiting out of the black community, who make up roughly 70% of the players in the NFL.

Most of the superstars and household names of the league are black. Of the 88 players who played in the 2021 Pro Bowl 66 were black. Meaning roughly 75% of the best players in the NFL are black. Numbers are similar when you compare the NFL to the NBA. Roughly 80% of the players in the NBA today are black, generating the majority of the income for the NBA, especially when we talk about the household names.

Final minutes of the 2020 NBA All-Star Game

In the 2020 All-Star Game, of the 24 NBA players who were invited, 21 were black. Black athletes in general have always been sought-after and considered the cream of the crop in almost every sport, yet we don't understand how powerful we are. Imagine as a unit if all black athletes got on code. The code would be simple. To refuse to put a game before your people. Meaning you should not give a damn about sports when it comes to the welfare of your fellow black brother and sister or the community as a whole. Let me paint a picture of how this would work.

Colin Kaepernick takes a knee for the unarmed killing of black men, women, and children at the hands of the police. He is bashed and demonized by the media, which in the system of white supremacy is to be expected. In response to the treatment of our brother we form a sort of organization for all black athletes in each particular sport. For example, let's just call it the UBA (United Black Athletes). An organization that represents all athletes in any professional sport, as well as being politically and socially aware of what is going on in the greater black community to shed light and create change to the situation.

As an organization speaking with all the black athletes in the NFL. The UBA reaches a decision that we will all take a knee for the anthem because that is not only what we feel is best for all black athletes, but the community as a whole. The organization puts out a statement that all players of black descent will be kneeling during the national anthem as a form of protest against police brutality and in support of our brother Colin Kaepernick's original stance. This would be the one and only statement we put out as an organization, that's it. No explaining, no arguing, because the oppressor is in no moral position to tell the oppressed how to protest.

Understand that the mainstream media is going to try to flip and make it about disrespecting the troops, that's fine. Let the white supremacist media do what they do. Now let's say in a perfect world every black player in the NFL ensues in taking a knee with our brother Colin Kaepernick. That's roughly 70% of the NFL. This forces the NFL to deal with the situation rather than blow it over and make it about Colin Kaepernick. The season goes by and we continue to stay on code until we see tangible change and justice granted to the black community. Whether it be a preseason, play off, or pro Bowl game, even the Super Bowl, we stay on code, as a backlash when the season ends as it did last year.

Owners from around the league as well as the members from the dominant society decided to target the supposed ringleader of the protest, Colin Kaepernick, as they did during the 2017 - 2018 season, blackballing him by making sure he never got another chance to play in the league again for exercising his first amendment right. The intent on why the NFL owners are blackballing him is clear, because in their eyes he was a slave who got out of line. It was clearly not from a talent standpoint as many of the white media portrayed it to be. Speaking from a football perspective Colin Kaepernick is the same player who took the league by storm and came up one play short of bringing home a Super Bowl trophy in 2013. Colin is also the same man who has the second-best pass to interception ratio in NFL history, only behind future Hall-of-Famer Aaron Rodgers.

Knowing these things as black players in the league, it would be our responsibility to say if he doesn't play this season, we won't. That's right, the same way the NFL owners try to make a statement by hitting Colin Kaepernick in his pockets. We can return the favor by hitting them and theirs. We're talking about 70% of the NFL's players vanishing overnight. Let's see how long owners around the league stay on the code of blackballing Colin Kaepernick. You have Jerry Jones of the Dallas Cowboys, who demanded his players stand for the national anthem.

It's your job as black men to make him put his money where his mouth is. There were 38 black players on the 2017 active roster. Now if you know anything about football you know only 53 players dress out. Meaning that if every African player challenged Jerry Jones on his word, there would only be 15 players left on the active roster. Not even enough to have two separate sides of the ball. We are talking about tens of millions of dollars walking out the door. Not to mention the loss in ticket sales and merchandise because nobody is going to come to the game and watch guys who were signed off the streets play.

You know what makes you lose money faster than protesting the anthem? losing. People come to the game in hopes of their team winning. If we come together like this on code, Colin Kaepernick would have a job in the NFL within a matter of 24 hours. Owners wouldn't care if you did the Tootsie Roll during the anthem, as long as you play so they can keep their money. This type of unity reform goes for any sport, men, or women. Dollars would stop flowing if we stopped providing our services. The little chump change they give our black athletes is pennies compared to what they're making for doing nothing but exploiting our talents.

As blacks in America, we're going to have to start throwing our weight around, like every other community does when they're in power. We must be willing to sacrifice some money for the greater good of the community. It's important to remember it's not just about professional sports where black athletes dominate, but amateur sports as well. We've heard the term million-dollar slave before as it applies to professional athletes. However, for our collegiate athletes, the simple term slave will suffice, all working a central job with no pay.

The NCAA is an empire built on America's favorite pastime, and the foundation in which this country was built on, slavery. Before we go any further, we already know we're going to have some Negro naysayers now saying, "the NCAA is not slavery they're getting their education paid for and they're just amateurs". Well, if that's the case, anybody who has anything to do with college athletics should not be paid.

Coaches, training staff, athletic directors, etc. If you are coaching amateurs that should make you an amateur. So instead of paying these coaches, they should get a meal plan, a place to stay, and a free education, but no pay.

Do you see how crazy that sounds? This is what we tell collegiate athletes every day. For example, football and basketball. You can't even come out of high school and go straight to the league. They make you go be a slave first, then feed you a lie, saying it's for the athlete's own well-being and health. Yet they will allow an 18-year-old kid to pick up a gun and go fight a war and call that patriotism. Look at the collegiate sports like football and basketball, two sports dominated by black players.

Alabama player Alex Leatherwood holding up 2021 National Championship trophy with Nick Saban

The recruiting for the two sports is nothing but modern-day slave auctions. Take college football for example which is heavily dominated by black players. In the 2017 ESPN top 300 which measures the top 300 High School football players entering the college ranks the next year of those players 240 of the 300 were black. That's 80% of the top football players going into college the next year. Do want to know something even crazier? all 240 black players listed in that ESPN top 300 committed to historically white schools.

Schools like Ohio State, Georgia, Ole Miss, Michigan etc. All schools that are historically white. Looking at their football teams however, they ironically look like HBCU's. Look at the 2017 national championship game between Alabama and Clemson where 18 out of the 22 starters on offense and defense for Alabama were black and 16 out of 22 starters on the offense and defense for Clemson where black. Yet only 10.4% of the students at the University of Alabama are black, and only 6.8% of the students at the University of Clemson are black according to 2017 statistics. These schools not football programs, don't give a damn about the black man in America, unless it benefits them financially.

Dabo Swinney, Clemson's head football coach is the same one who said, *"we have a sin problem in this world not a racial one"*, because we have a black president, black CEOs, interracial couples etc. This is the mindset a lot of these white coaches past and present like Dabo Swinney and even Lou Holtz has. Holt's former head coach of Notre Dame, a Christian school I might add, when asked what he would do if one of his star players kneeled for the national anthem, responded by saying this, *"he wouldn't be a star player any longer, because we are not going to use this football team to promote any political causes only thing you're here to do is promote this university"*. I guess in Christianity a game is more important than black lives. These college football schools and coaches make it clear you are here to play football, take this scholarship and shut up. A scholarship that is essentially worthless compared to the profits black players bring into the school.

For example, back to Alabama and Clemson, the 18 out of 22 black starters on the 2016/2017 Alabama football team. The university roughly spent $815,688 on their tuition combined last year. Of all the 85 full scholarship players on Alabama's team last year, the university spent a little over 3.9 million, including housing, meals etc. That might sound like a lot of money but it's nothing compared to what they made off them. In the 2016-2017 football season, the Alabama program brought in an incredible 108.1 million dollars.

That's right, in one single year, which they only technically spent roughly 3% of their earnings on the players on full scholarship. To the 16 out of 22 Black starters on the 2016-2017 Clemson football team, they roughly spent about $776,704 on their tuitions combined that year. Of all the 85 full scholarship players on Clemson's football team the university spent a little over

4.1 million combined, on housing, meals etc. Again, it might sound like a lot but it's not. In the 2016/2017 season Clemson football brought in 45.9 million. Even though that's less than half of what Alabama brought in, that's still a hell of a return, considering the fact that they only had to pay about 8% of their earnings to their 85 full scholarship players in tuition.

In other words, in the case of schools such as Alabama and Clemson, over 90% of the profits these football programs produce, go to someone other than the players. Yet the players are the only ones putting their lives and futures on the line. These are not just isolated incidents; this is pretty much the case in all power 5 schools at least. The university make so much and give the players crumbs because they claim them to be amateurs. You will find the same thing in college basketball as well.

According to the ESPN's top 100 high school basketball players in 2017, 93 out of the top 100 players were black. That's right 93%, and just like the recruits in high School football every last one of them committed to a historically white school. Schools such as Kentucky, Duke, North Carolina etc. Schools you will find out are historically white colleges in the classroom, but historically black on the court. In 2016 the Kansas Jayhawks basketball team brought in 16.1 million dollars of revenue. The Kentucky Wildcats in 2016 brought in 25.1 million dollars in revenue. The North Carolina Tar Heels brought in 19.5 million dollars in revenue. The Duke Blue Devils brought in 31.2 million dollars in revenue. These are just to name a few from the most recent study done in 2016.

All of these teams are made up of mostly black players. Now many of you are still wondering, how can our collegiate athlete help the black community if they can't get paid? It's a good question with a simple answer. Your decision on what school to attend is payment, an economic investment into the black community. I just showed you how much money black athletes are generating for these historically white schools, which tallies in the hundreds of millions.

We must start instilling in our young athletes the priority on attending and bringing this money to HBCU's. Many of the HBCUs in America is in financial crisis. Years of falling enrollment, stringing endowments, poor management etc., have caused many to question such institutions staying power. According to a 2016 study, today only about 10% of black college students attend historically black schools, a number that started declining due to the desegregation in the school system. As a result, HBCUs have essentially lost the black dollar.

For example, in 2015 Moody's investor service cut the credit rating of Howard University, one of the country's premier HBCUs for the third time since 2013 and labelled it a substantial credit risk. Morris Brown College is another extreme example of a HBCU in dire financial need. In 2003 Morris Brown had an enrollment of 2700 students. Today it only has about 40 students.

Possibly by the time you read this book it might be closed.

The fact is Morris Brown and Howard are some of more than 100 HBCUs grappling severe levels of debt. Now can you imagine what a huge economic boost it would be if we had the top black athletes in the country come to HBCUs? It would shift the whole economic picture of collegiate sports. Our young brothers on the football field at Alabama and Clemson who help to bring in hundreds of millions of dollars for their university could do the same for HBCUs. Black athletes have the chance to change this by bringing advertisements, endorsements, bowl money etc., to HBCUS, by simply attending and playing for them.

Not only will you be boosting the school but the black community around the school as well, by bringing people from all over the state and country to see the best of the best play. In return it will create a massive flow of money into the local black community and businesses, causing the black dollar in our community to bounce, all of this because of our black athletes taking their talents to black colleges. This is something I want all my young athletes to think about if you are serious about helping the black community. If the NCAA is not going to pay you like they should, you might as well have your labor benefit the black community who are in desperate need of help, because something that history has proven is no matter what school you go to, the NFL, the NBA, the MLB etc. will always find you. Yes, you might have to sacrifice some of the limelight and notoriety, but let your sacrifice be the foundation of the future success to come.

Let them say 10 years from now that you were the first ESPN top 10 recruit to attend a HBCU straight out of high school, and because of that decision you created the great success that followed for HBCU programs in the 10 years after that. Look at all the money that is now flowing into HBCUs because of the rebirth of the top black athletes at those schools. Look at the thriving communities that now surround the school because of the money the players help to bring in on Saturdays and Sundays throughout the week. In closing, just like I challenge all black people to bank black and buy black, I challenge all of my young high school and collegiate athletes to attend black colleges, in order to make a more positive change and impact on our communities.

Great NFL running backs past and present. Walter Payton (Left) and Tarik Cohen (Right) two HBCU products.

Powernomics

Throughout this section we have learned ways to

make money, keep money and empower our community with it. Yet, the big question that still remains is how do we structure this new form of economic thinking in order to implement power? In comes the *"Powernomics"* concept introduced by Dr. Claud Anderson. *"Powernomics"* includes five categories' Economics, Politics, Courts/Police, Media, and Education. These are the five floors of *"Powernomics"*.

The 5 levels of Powernomics

Starting with the first and most important floor economic empowerment. Racism is economics, the reason why they beat up on us now is because they know we have no economic system. When you see these race soldiers out here shooting black people it's because they know you're powerless, meaning we have no power and wealth. Therefore, it's important for us as stated before, to bank black. It is the black bank that creates the foundation for our powernomics concept that we are attempting to implement.

In the powernomics concept the black bank's job is to offer access to capital for up-and-coming black businesses who would otherwise receive no capital. In return the black businesses use this money to grow and scale, providing well needed jobs, and income for members of the black community. Then as a business owner you take the surplus capital that you've built from the support of the community (see Buying Black section) and move to the next floor of the powernomics chain which is politics. Quit believing the LIE people constantly tell us that the only way to make a change is through voting. Child please. Voting isn't worth anything if you don't have an economy.

Now you take that money that we've gained off the first floor and use it to buy every politician on the second floor. As Dr. Claud Anderson says, *"don't worry about voting, buy them"*. Did you see the Chinese community on the corner last presidency election talking about voting? What about the Jewish community or the East Indian community? Wonder why?

They don't vote for politicians they just buy them. Even if we don't have enough money to buy them rent or lease them for a while. After you've paid them off or put them under lease for a certain amount of time, we then put them to work for the black community. Make the politicians you bought go to work for you on the third level, which is the justice system. Therefore, the politicians, the ones who control and implement the laws, can put in policies and laws to stop the killings of unarmed black men, women, and children at the hands of the cops, along with other things we see fit for our agenda. Understand that when I say buy them, I mean buy the politicians at every level, the national level, state level, and the local level.

In return for our money these court systems will fall in favor of our interest more, especially on the local levels, where our money will have more impact. How many times have you heard about police shooting down Chinese, Jewish, or Arab people? Almost never, and when it does happen the cop is immediately held accountable. It's a result of these communities controlling the local court system in policing in their area. Now once we begin to do this, we take our money and move to the 4th floor which is the media. How in the world can we communicate, or mobilize our people when we own little to no media outlets?

Studies show that mass media through our television sets are the most popular form of leisure time activities. Most TVs are often on up to eight hours a day. With the average viewer watching more than 28 hours of television every week. Out of these 28 hours of television every week, what images are they being fed of the black man and woman? Images full of propaganda with shows like Ancient Aliens teaching our children that Aliens built the pyramids or news outlets portraying us as thugs and criminals or trying to convince us to be guinea pigs for vaccines.

The only time we're spoken about in a positive manner is when they're praising one of our athletes and even then, most times that's for cooning. Again, the reason why we never see positive images of us is because we own little to no mainstream media outlets or any outlets in general. This is because we don't have the black businesses to support. This is why they can get rid of all our conscious brothers and sisters who might get on TV and take a stand against white supremacy. At the same time, these same white businesses will allow these white supremacists on TV such as the Rush Limbaughs, Sean Hannity, or Tucker Carlson. This is because they have the advertising dollar of the white businesses who support them.

On the flip side of that it also goes back to supporting black businesses as we discussed earlier. We as black people give these white businesses the money to support the white supremacist news anchors. I see black people all the time complaining about what a certain news network said about our people, but yet tune in the next day to watch that same show. By doing so they continue to support those businesses who are sponsoring that show. When are we as black people going to start renegotiating our relationship with these companies? by putting our foot down and saying to them, *"if we see you supporting negative news and stories about black people you will never get another dollar out of the black community again".* None of that 1.2 trillion dollars of spending power will ever see your company.

That goes for anybody, negroes included, who are shucking and jiving for the dominant society, implying that in any regard black people are lazy, dumb, criminal, terroristic or stupid, we will shut off every dollar coming into your company or personal account. The companies who support these white supremacists are not scared of us, therefore they take our money for granted. This is why it is important to have our own black media that is sponsored by black dollars, to let our people know what the truth is, and how we should respond and react to it as a unit. With our own news outlets, we can convince our people to vote for neither the Republic nor the Democratic Party come election time. Thus, forming our own Independent Party as black people.

We allow these news outlets to manipulate our minds into who we're going to vote for. If you watch Fox News all day, they're going to convince you that voting for a Republican is what's best for you. If you watch CNN, they're going to convince you that voting for a Democrat is what's best for you, when we know based on history, neither is what's best for us. Just two fangs off the same snake. We need black media outlets to spread this message.

The only way to do this is by starting and owning our own media companies that will look out for the best interests of our people or at least controlling the sponsorship dollars on other outlets through our businesses. Now that we have discussed the first four floors, there is only one left, the 5th floor, which is education. All the floors lead to the education floor, whether it be just knowing thyself or financial literacy. Education is the key to our future as a people. Now we must understand one thing. Education is about as useless as the black vote if you don't have an economy.

What's the point of going to school for 8 years and getting your doctorate degree only to turn right around and use it to empower white folks or to be boycotted because of racism in the corporate world. All the degrees black people in America have, yet still have to go and beg another community for a job. When the Chinese man or woman finishes school, they know they can go straight back to their community and get a job, if not open their own business with the support of their community. Again, I reiterate when speaking from an economic standpoint, education is nothing without having your own economy. 2016 studies done by EPI analysts still show that blacks who graduate with a college degree are still twice as unlikely to get a job than whites with the same degree.

The same goes for blacks with a high school diploma, they are still twice as unlikely to end up with a job, then a white person with the same diploma. Now we know that race is playing a heavy role in the reason so many of our black college graduates are jobless, yet this is something that we have known for hundreds of years, but where are our black businesses to counter this discrimination? Where is our economic foundation to support our people with degrees? We would not have to worry about racial discrimination in the job market if we employed our own and started our own businesses. The fact is, in the real world you must have economies before education.

There is also another side of education that has an economic impact. The schools in themselves, especially our public schools, from elementary to high school. We must begin to build our own schools with our own independent educational curriculum. Within any fight for revolution and liberation, you cannot have your oppressors teaching your children. You cannot have your oppressor dictating what your children learn and not learn.

You cannot send children to the oppressor and expect them to come back with knowledge of self. It's just not going to happen. Please, don't get confused by the black face your child's teacher might have, thinking that since they're black they are teaching them how to be an independent free thinking black man or woman with a thorough knowledge of self. When most of the time the reality is, your kids are just being fed white supremacy through a black face. That's not to say that black teachers are bad people or purposely doing this.

As a matter of fact, I think they do an amazing job with our children, considering the circumstances and criteria they are required to teach. However, with that being said, you can be a good teacher, but just in a bad system, which is the case here in the United States that has practically coined the term school-to-prison pipeline, a disturbing national trend where children are funneled out of public school and into the juvenile and criminal justice system. Many of these children in the black community have learning disabilities or are of poverty, abuse, or neglect, and would benefit from additional education and counseling services. Instead, they are isolated, punished, and pushed out. Put on drugs like Ritalin or Adderall, with doctors calling it, Attention Deficit Disorder (ADD) or Attention Deficit Hyperactivity Disorder (ADHD).

What they don't tell you is that the drugs they're giving your kids are in the same family as drugs such as cocaine and meth. The only difference is that Ritalin and Adderall are served by your local pharmacist instead of your local drug dealer. More and more of our young children are getting prescribed and put on these crack-like drugs at a young age. Counselors and pharmacists alike, taking advantage of ill-informed parents who feel that drugging their kids is the best thing for their future, when in fact it's not that your child is suffering from a disorder, it's just your child is being a child. Go online and look up some of the symptoms of what they would call ADHD. For example, one of the symptoms states from a behavior standpoint, children might experience excitability, fidgeting hyperactivity, impulsiveness, and lack of restraint. Really! this is describing every kid in America.

What kid isn't always fidgeting and messing with something? What kid isn't excitable, impulsive, or hyperactive? They are kids, that's why people always say you have to watch your kids. ADHD says your kids will have difficulty focusing, problems paying attention, or have a short attention span. Again really! do you know a kid that just sits in one spot all day? What kid do you know that just focuses on one thing?

Watch any kid play today, they play with a different toy every 5 minutes. These actions are nothing out of the normal for a child, yet it gets better. It also says children with ADHD will be angry or excited and/or have mood swings. Come on now my brothers and sisters, again we're smarter than this. We call these actions in the black households temper tantrums. My sister and I used to have them all the time as a kid. You know what the remedy was for that growing up in my family and a lot of yours'? Getting popped on the butt or put in timeout.

Ironically after that, magically somehow, we just stopped acting up with the quickness. It's that simple. It's part of growing up as a child, you have to learn that it's certain things you can't do or there will be consequences for those actions. It also takes good parents to realize that these behavioral traits of your child don't mean that anything is wrong with them. It's just a child being a child. These crack like substances such as Ritalin and Adderall prescribed by doctors are not the way to solve those issues. Our brother Dr. Umar Johnson has a great book *"Psycho Academic Holocaust: The special education ADHD war against black boys"* educating parents on how to fight back against counselors and doctors trying to put your children on those prescription drugs. Dr. Umar Johnson describes ADHD as nothing but the *"ain't no Daddy at home disorder"*.

Seeming that most of the children who are targeted for ADHD are young black males who are raised in the household with single mothers, only acting out from the lack of love from a dominant male figure in their life. This is why on the 5th floor of powernomics we must use our own economy to build our own schools, because most of the time, these drugs and disorders are prescribed to our children from schools and teachers alike. Intuitions and people who simply don't know how to handle black kids. So, to be clear, I'm not talking about a charter school because charter schools are still public schools by law. Meaning the local and state departments of education can still dictate the curriculum, and school culture.

We need private schools, which in return will be tougher because we will have to raise our own funds. However, with the mental fortitude and buying power we have, we can do so, that way, we can dictate the curriculum and culture at our school, resulting in strong black men and women who know truth history and what they have to do for their community at a young age. These are the five floors of powernomics that we must master in the black community if we're going to survive. Participating in group economics is not a matter of hate for others, it's a matter of love for ourselves.

Conclusion

In conclusion, I hope that by now you understand from reading this section that you cannot have black power without the black dollar. We must begin as a community to understand how money works and how to effectively use it to our good. Black economic empowerment has to be the quintessential cornerstone to our communities. Everything goes hand-in-hand, from financial literacy and understanding the power of investments to black financial institutions themselves knowing the powerful role they play in the building of our community. Black economic empowerment is a simple plan that can be easily executed if we just make up our minds to stop being consumers and start being owners.

Owners of our Economy, Politics, Education, and our livelihood in general. When we do these things, we will become without question, the most powerful group in not only the United States but the world, because remember, Powernomics is just like any other game. The goal is not to play a close game or play a draw, the goal is to win and in the words of Dr. Kaba Kamene *"It ain't over until we WIN."*

Part. 3

The Art of Defense

***"I do not even call it violence when it is
self-defense; I call it intelligence"***

- Malcolm X

Finally, we have reached the last key part of the
Voice of the Ancestors series and if you haven't noticed
by now, you come from a magnificent group of people, a
people that have embodied everything that is great about
humanity and who everyone owes their cultures, arts,
sciences, and civilizations too, that we are Gods walking
this very earth, having a human experience. As you have
learned, we are also Gods who have been so spoiled by
our abilities as a people, that we have forgotten the first
rule of survival, which is the art of defense. If we are to

reach the level of excellence we once possessed as a
people, we must learn to defend it or risk losing it again.
Our mistakes of the past have cost us our knowledge of
self, tradition, culture, and way of life. Yet despite this,
words like defense, military strategy, fighting back, are
words and phrases that in some degree seem to be
forbidden in the black community.

As I have preached to you throughout the book, we
have been taught to be submissive, a theme that has been
taught to us since grade school, all the way into college
and thereafter, enforced in many of our churches and
other institutions of worship. A global society and system
that has taught the African that if someone steals your
land you don't take it back, you pray for it back and offer
to share it with the people who stole it. They have
ingrained in our minds that if our people are being killed
unjustly, you don't respond with acts of violence, you
march and peacefully protest and hope that change one
day will come. The dominant society tells us that you
can't gain freedom and liberation through the methods of
a Malcolm X or Dedan Kimathi, that the right way to
achieve what you want is through the methods of Martin
Luther King Jr. or Medgar Edgar's. Yet when you think
about it, what has the system of white supremacy ever let
us achieve in the first place by any method.

Not to mention the last time I checked, everyone I
just mentioned that society said did it the wrong or the
right way, was murdered. Killed by the system of white
supremacy and its soldiers who work so hard to enforce
it. Where does that leave us as black people, do we

continue to lay back and let our oppressors decide the right way to achieve our freedom or defend ourselves? For those of us still on the fence, let me ask you this, is the way the dominant society expects and tells us to act the same way they act towards us? Think about it, when a white person dies on any corner of the earth for something members and his community feel was unjust, that community goes to war.

This is the same country that picked up arms because they felt they were being overtaxed by the British. Yet the same country turns around today and tells you and I not to fight back when the blood of your people is spilled in the streets. Do you see the irony in that? I do, which is why in this chapter we're going to learn about things they don't teach you in school. Such as the art of the defense itself. Yet from a chess point of view, meaning strategy, because remember, if you're going to defend yourself and your people in the system of white supremacy it requires you to play chess. So, we're not just going to dive into the art of defense as it pertains to physical warfare, but we are going to discuss the art of defense as it pertains to our mental and financial skills as well, because it is important that we learn how to defend every structure of our nation with absolute precision and certainty. The time for hiding is over, it's time to fight back.

OGUN

In order to understand the art of defense, you must first know the warrior within. Known in the Yoruba and Vodun spiritual systems as Ogun, this is a warrior spirit that lives in us all. One doesn't summon it when they want to be peaceful or diplomatic, one only summons it in times of war and my brothers and sisters, I'm here to tell you, we are at war, yet most of us are in denial of it because we fear it. We fear war because we don't know our history. One thing our oppressor has done is only educate us on history of when he was victorious, and we were defeated. Times where he was brave and courageous, and we were scared and submissive.

As a result, in 2021 many of us suppress the Ogun energy for fear it won't be good enough, and we won't win. But the facts are we have lost some battles but when on code have always won the wars. We won with some of the most courageous and skillful soldiers the world has ever seen, who's legacies live on even till this day. For example, let's start in ancient times with Nubia. One of the earliest names for Nubia given to them by the Kemites was Ta-Seti, meaning the "Land of the Bow."

A name that signified to all that the people of the land were not to be played with when it came to warfare as they were excellent archers. These Nubians were so good with the bow and arrow that in instances, the Kemites would hire them to help defend their land in times of war. Nubian archers were one of the main reasons foreign invaders could not fully conquer pass Kemet, as in the 8th century, Nubian archers fought back Muslim invaders. In their account of the event, the Muslims noted the accuracy of Nubian arrows that drove them away. However, although their brothers and sisters to the north needed help at times, the Kemites weren't too shabby themselves when it came to military warfare.

After all you don't have a flourishing civilization that lasted for thousands of years without a powerful military force. The Kemites defeated several invaders during their time including the Hyksos, Assyrians, and even the Nubians in instances, doing so with advanced weapons such as heavily armed chariots, and at their height a standing army of over a hundred thousand men wielding bronze tipped spears and javelins.

***Depiction of Battle with the Nubians: This painting shows
Ramses II battling Nubians from his war chariot.***

Even after the fall of civilization in antiquity
northeast Africa has been a very difficult place for
foreign invaders to colonize. You have brothers like
Mohammad Ahmad, known as the first Mahdi of Sudan,
who defeated every army that England sent against him,
one of which was 11,000 strong. At the time of his death
in 1885, he had carved out an empire that stretched 1600
miles long and 700 miles wide. He was the man who
killed the famous English General "Chinese" Gordon.
Just to the east of Mohammad Ahmad during the same
time period, you had another warrior king named
Menelik II. A man who is said to be the father of
modern-day Ethiopia, mainly due to his military victories

over the Italians.

Menelik II and the Arbegnoch soldiers that came after him are a big reason why even to this day Ethiopia has never been colonized. Moving out towards west Africa you not only see the men playing a prominent role in defense, but the women as well. Women such as Seh-Dong-Hong-Beh, who was a leader of an all-woman army known as the Dahomey Mino (Amazons), that at one time had over 6,000 women. She was one of the last soldiers in a 200 plus-year succession that helped to defend the powerful Dahomey empire. Yet, Seh-Dong-Hong-Beh was not the first woman warrior in west African history.

Women such as Queen Amina were fierce in their own right as she ruled over the Zazzau city-states in what is now modern-day Nigeria. Her army consisted of 20,000 soldiers who were as well trained and fearsome as her. One of her first announcements to her people as Queen was a call for them to "resharpen their weapons." Resharpen their weapons they did as her army conquered large portions of land across Nigeria. Then you have brothers like Hannibal in the north and Shaka Zula in the south. Each from a different time period in African history, but powerful military Generals who went toe to toe with some of the biggest world powers of their times.

Seh-Dong-Hong-Beh, drawn by Frederick Forbes, 1851

As you're reading this, I want to be sure to point out however that these were not just isolated incidents on the continent of Africa. As you know by now, we are a global people and as a result fought back to defend ourselves as well as others around the world from times of antiquity until now. Moors such as General Tariq had great victories in southern Iberia, most notably being in the battle of Guadalete where he defeated King Roderic. This victory opened the door for Moorish enlightenment in the region, helping to bring Europe out of the dark ages. It was a black man in Russia named Ivan Gannibal who helped the Russians fight off the Ottoman empire due to his courageous acts on the seas. Gannibal received the "Order of St. George" for his contributions during the war, which is the highest military honor one can receive in Russia. In later years he became a very powerful man, owning vast estates and even becoming one of the founding fathers of Kherson.

Over in Asia you had powerful brothers all over who excelled in warfare like Malik Ambar of India, David Fagen of the Philippines, and Yasuke the Black Samurai. There is even a Japanese proverb that states *"For a samurai to be brave, he must have a bit of black blood."* The same warrior energy can be found down in Australia among the Aborigines, who defended their land against colonization with their life. Pemulwuy is regarded among many scholars and historians as one of the greatest resisters against colonization. In Port Jackson in 1790 he speared John McIntyre who was at the time one of the biggest terrorists of the aborigines. McIntyre later died of his injuries. Thereafter from the year 1790 – 1802 Pemulwuy engaged in a 12-year guerrilla warfare with the British before he was killed. His efforts inspired many including Yagan, Musquito, Jandamarra and more who led resistance movements against the British in the decades after.

Pemulwuy, Aboriginal resistance leader - bronze sculpture by Masha Marjanovich

Yagan statue, Heirisson Island

In the Americas it was no different, from the first

time Europeans attempted to enslave black people we fought back and won. In fact, historians and scholars rarely talk about the fate of the very first European settlement on the north American continent known as San Miguel de Gualdape, located in now modern-day Georgia. It was at this site in 1526 that Spanish explorer Lucas Vazquez, along with other settlers would be killed by the very Africans they were attempting to enslave. This was the first of many slave revolts over the centuries that followed. Even during the civil rights movement, you had events such as the long hot summer of 1967, where there were over 200 racial riots in black cities around America.

As a result, many key civil rights acts were put into place the following year. Honestly family, I can go on for pages about the warrior spirit we possess, yet the main point I want you take away from this is that we have always fought and resisted. Therefore, when we are looking for the heart or courage to fight back and defeat our oppressors we must look within. For Ogun is not this magical spirit outside of you, Ogun is you. The bodies our ancestors left behind are proof of that.

Weaponizing the Mind

As stated, before history is something that we as Black people must study and learn more from. The reason being that history always repeats itself. Most times taking us from point A to point B through the same process it took us 400 years ago. Now when we look at history in terms of warfare it's the same. Before there is any form of physical warfare, there is psychological warfare. I would even argue that the mind is the most important part of war.

Understand, the most important organ in our bodies is our mind. Your mind controls all the functions in your body, as well as interpreting information from the outside world. For example, any doctor will tell you there are three stages of thought your mind goes through. That would be your conscious, subconscious, and unconscious thoughts. Now all three parts work together on a daily basis to perform your everyday tasks and help you to overcome those day-to-day obstacles. Whether successful or not, that depends on how you use your brain.

Now imagine your mind is like a computer. Your conscious mind is therefore best represented by the keyboard, mouse, and the monitor. You input data on the keyboard and results come up on the screen. So, your conscious mind takes information you have fed it, and instantaneously gives you the result of the information. Your subconscious is like the ram in your computer, where it programs the data that is currently in use and keeps it stored, so that it can easily be reached quickly by your computer processor, in this case your conscious mind.

The subconscious stores those recent memories such as your name, telephone number, or what you ate today. Your unconscious on the other hand is like the hard disk in your computer. It is a long-term storage place for all your memories and programs that have been installed in it since birth. Now ultimately, you're unconscious and your subconscious mind use their powers to make sense of all the data they receive from the conscious, in order to keep you safe and ensure your survival. Now for the question many of you are asking right now, why is this important? Why is it so important I understand how my brain works?

Well, it is important to know because our mind, just like a computer, can be programmed to do anything. Like a computer, it does not ask whether the information you are uploading is for the good or for the bad, it just uploads the information. Your brain is like a computer or fertile soil, whatever seed is allowed to be planted in it will grow. Unfortunately for many of us black people, a virus has been planted and programed into our soil and/or computer, spreading like the plague from one black person to another. This is what happens in the computing world when you don't put firewalls in your computer, anything can grow and spread.

This is the reason why we are in the condition we

are in today. Because as great as our ancestors were both intellectually and spiritually, one thing they consistently failed to do throughout their years was weaponize their minds. This is how the system of white supremacy came into power in the first place by simply weaponizing the mind. For example, in the mythological *"Willie Lynch Letter: How to make African-American slaves for 1000 years"* a white supremacist name Willie Lynch told an audience full of slave owners how to control and make a Slave. Now again the story was made up but the message in it was real.

Lynch said *"Hence, both the horse and the Niger must be broken; that is breaking them from one form of mental life to another. Keep the body, take the mind! In other words, break the will to resist".* You see Willie Lynch, just like the white supremacists today, understood that if you take the mind the body will follow. From a global view this is the only way a minority group of people being white, could control the majority group of people, being melanated. Again, what we have today is a lot of black people who have been programmed in the white man's image. That's why they can continue to kill, rape, and steal from our people without any fear of repercussions. The virus has already been downloaded on our hard disk drive being the unconscious part of our mind.

So, the utter thought of resistance or fighting back essentially becomes impossible for you to carry out. Just like your computer can't disobey a direct order because it's been programmed not to. This is where we stand, in today's time with the greatest most powerful force the world has ever seen, the black mind being controlled and manipulated by someone other than itself. Now the question becomes where does that leave us? How can we take back and control the most powerful force on the face of the earth?

One way is by re-educating ourselves on our history as stated before in the OGUN section. Yet we also must keep in mind, the same way you upload firewall protection to get rid of the virus on your computer, is the same way you have to upload truth to get rid of the lies in your mind. But first let me say this before I go any further. We need to understand that unfortunately some black people are too far gone, meaning the virus that has been uploaded into their mind is too deep to control at this point. Most times these are our elders in the community and even some of our younger brothers and sisters.

There is no point in arguing with these individuals because their mind is made up. Most of the time you can tell this by the way they deny every string of evidence you present before them, content to just believe the lies they have been told. This is okay though, by no way does this mean we ridicule our brothers and sisters who are lost. We will still continue to treat them like the kings and queens they are, but at the same time, we cannot waste time with individuals who are not mentally stable enough to accept and understand the truth. Just wish those brothers and sisters in our community hotep and keep it moving.

Now on a progressive note, to those in our community who showed the mental fortitude to want to reprogram their self, it's a simple two-step process. First, just like you would reprogram your computer, you reprogram your mind by shutting down and starting it over from scratch, erasing the sources in which you normally get your information, until these sources of information and education are thoroughly reviewed to make sure they are factual. This is the same way you erase all the spam and pop-up ads from your computer. Because in the computer, just like the mind, you will find a lot of times that the virus itself came through the spam mail and pop-up ads. Remember from the standpoint of your mind, the source in which it gathers information can be from anywhere, internet, school, books, people etc. That's why it's important to erase them all until they can be examined thoroughly.

After you have shut down and reprogrammed your mind, you want to move on to the second step, which is to begin accepting knowledge again. Only this time use what I like to call the Matrix effect. The Matrix effect is simple, you have to assume it's everywhere around you and in every part of your day-to-day life. When you look outside your window it's there. When you turn on the TV it's there. You can sense it when you go to work, church, or pay the government taxes.

The Matrix is the lies that have been embedded in your mind, to blind you from the truth that you are programmed. That you are a slave. It's like a community of viruses in your computer, all linked to each other to make one another stronger. As a result, what you have is a lie protecting another lie protecting another lie. Therefore, it's important that we understand how the Matrix works and operates, in order to expose it for what it is.

This is where weaponizing your mind comes in. I want you from now on to treat your mind as if it were your own baby and the most precious thing in the world. Therefore, in order to protect it, every piece of information or education that tries to enter it must be put on hold until thoroughly examined. I do not care who it is coming from, whether it's the school system, the church, or the President. Weaponizing the mind will allow you to shoot down the lies that attempt to put a virus in your mind and throw you back into the Matrix. You must put a filter or force field around your mind where only truth gets through.

This truth is based on the facts and evidence that has been backed by scientific research and double-checked by your own research. This truth is not based from faith or somebody's word because these are things that can easily be lies and discredited through research. For example, lies such as Christopher Columbus discovered America will no longer even be entertained in our mind based from the evidence and scientific research done by others including yourself. However, as stated before destroying one lie does not mean you've destroyed the Matrix. For the Matrix uses a multitude of lies to protect previous lies.

So, anybody with common sense knows by now he didn't discover America. Yet most of us will settle for the lie used to cover it, which is that the Indians with the Mongolian phenotype, who migrated over the Bering straits more than 12,000 years ago, are the first people of America, when that too is a lie based on scientific evidence and research as we discussed in Part 1. By denying one lie and settling for another is still allowing the virus to enter the mind, essentially keeping you in the Matrix? That's why it must be determined that based on scientific evidence and research the information you are allowing to enter your mind is facts. For many of us that's why we must shut down and reprogram our minds, then use the Matrix effect to defend it.

It's important to note though, whenever you talk about building a nation, one of the main if not the top concerns is the future of that nation, referring to the children who will be in charge of carrying the torch of the empire. I bring this up because as I mentioned earlier, many of our people unfortunately will never get out of the Matrix, because they are too deep into it to be pulled out. The question that we should be asking is why? Why they are at the point of no recovery, no matter what evidence is presented to them or what research they discover for their self. They will never believe anything besides the LIE they were told at the beginning. The reason being, as research has shown for decades, there is an extraordinary development of the brain between the ages of 0 and 5, according to the Wisconsin council on children and families, Children are essentially born with a blank slate ready to learn.

Children cultivate 85% of their intellect, personality, and skill by the age of five. These first months and years of their life set the stage for the child's lifelong development. With the Neuroscience in the new millennium, it actually takes up to 12 years for the brain to become fully organized through the later teen years. That means that by the time your child is 12 he or she has already developed a priority list on a need and want basis, as well as an understanding of their environment, and social construct, including the understanding of race and where their collective community fits in on the totem pole. Research done by Mahzarin Banaji, who is a renowned Harvard University Psychologist, stated that even though they may not understand the why of their feelings, children exposed to racism tend to accept and embrace it as young as age 3, and in just a matter of days.

Banaji adds by saying *"We have known for a very long time that children process information differently than adults. That is a given, but what has changed where racism and other prejudice is concerned, is that we had far over calculated how long it takes for these traits to become embedded in a child's brain. It's quite shocking really, but the gist of it is that three and four-year-olds demonstrate the same level and type of bias as adults. This tells us that children get it very quickly, and that it doesn't require a mature level cognition to form negative bias"*. You can see examples of this research through tests going as far back as the Kenneth and Clark Doll Experiment used in the 1954 Brown vs. Board of Education, proving separate public schools for black and white students to be unconstitutional. An experiment which proved in theory that if you take 25 little black girls from say Atlanta and gave them a white doll and a black doll, then ask them which one is ugly and which one is cute, the majority will say the black doll is ugly and the white one is cute. Meaning that not only does your child know about race and where they fit in via the dominant society through forms of social media, TV etcetera, but they also know how they are supposed to respond to it.

The dominant society programs the submissive Negro trait in them by the age of 12. Therefore, any form of the defense and resistance in the child has been taken out at a young age. This is the case with most of the elders and adults in the black community who I said to be a lost cause. It is important we solve this problem in the black community by building our own black or African-based culture schools and communities. As I stated earlier in Part 3, it is impossible to think we can send our children to a school run by the system of white supremacy and expect our children's not to be programmed into the Matrix. That's why when this fertile learning cycle is over and they are forced to try to step outside of the Matrix of Lies, they can't do it.

The lies have now become truth to them because that's what they were born and raised to believe and whoever tries to teach them otherwise is considered the devil. We must stop the virus before it even attempts to get started, and that my brothers and sisters starts with the school system, because once we take back our mind the body will follow.

Defending Your Assets

We went into great detail in part 2 about the importance of the black dollar in the black community. That essentially the economy is the backbone of any nation and the stronger and more organized the dollar in your community the better. Building our dollar is just the first part of the process, keeping it is the second part. Many would even argue it's both the hardest and the most important part, especially when we are coming from an individual standpoint. Because it's not just about gaining assets but defending those assets as well.

Let's start with one of the biggest threats in our community as far as maintaining our wealth goes. The transition of wealth from one generation to another. I'm not referring to the transition of wealth from one generation to another in the form of stocks, bonds, or real estate. I'm talking about the most basic form of transferring wealth, which is via life insurance. Now it's ironic that the simplest and easiest form of transferring wealth from one generation to another is also the most feared to talk about. Although according to research and studies 6 to 10 black American households indicate they are fairly or very likely to buy life insurance for themselves or another member within the next 12 months.

This is a number that we must raise considering the atrocities we have faced and still can face as a people in America. Often when the word life insurance is even mentioned in our community, we shut down or put the subject to the side in fear of thinking about dying. This is fear we must overcome for it is selfish to punish the ones we love because we don't want to address a certain issue. Life insurance is something Eugene Mitchell, Corporate Vice President and an African American Market Manager at New York Life says can help black people. See, life insurance is so much more than being about a quick fix. It helps to protect your assets, creating inheritance, and passing wealth on to the next generation.

Things to know about life insurance is that it provides many different levels of protection. Mortgage payments, college costs, along with other bills or expenses. Second thing that many people don't know is that it provides living benefits. You don't have to die to benefit from your life insurance policy. For example, in 2017 more than half of all black families in the United States had no retirement money or wealth at all. Meaning they will likely be entirely dependent on Social Security, now paying an average monthly benefit of just over $1,200.

The cash value on a whole life insurance policy

can be accessed as a savings vehicle with guarantees and tax advantages. Which means a 65-year-old client who has had a life insurance policy for their whole adult life could end up with enough money in cash value to act as a good source of income in retirement. The cash value can be accessed as a loan or a reduction of the death benefit. Last but not least life insurance helps protect your assets by adding to them, not taking away from them. Let's say the breadwinner of the family is lost and the mainstream of income stops. This is one of the biggest concerns in our community when most of the family's financial assets are lost or are completely depleted, due to the unfortunate fact that the person who happened to pass away was the heartbeat of the family's financial assets. Now the family's mood goes from wealth building to that of debt building.

A 2013 New York Life survey showed that most Americans on average want enough life insurance to pay expenses for at least 14 years after the loss of a breadwinner, but in reality, only have 3 years of protection in place. Now keep in mind if you don't have life insurance at all, you would be forced to start from scratch, attempting to find a new stream of income to replace the ones you lost. However, if a loved one passes away with life insurance, he or she's family could possibly receive up to $250,000 in benefits, giving their respective families the ability to generate new forms of income to replace the lost ones. $50,000 could be used for that family to invest in high-end dividend stocks that will grow slowly in interest as well as pay them monthly or quarterly just for having invested in stocks. They could also take that $250,000 and use it to make a purchase on a real estate investment in the area where gentrification is increasing the property values. These are the many advantages of having life insurance that will help to protect assets and also build them.

Too many times in our community we are losing our assets because the person who acquired them died. This is something that has to stop. Life insurance has to be number one on our to do list when it comes to protecting our assets. Now that we have discussed and understand the most basic form of protecting our assets, let's go deeper. One of the major keys to defending your assets is understanding the environment they are in and what is the most immediate and dangerous threats to your wealth. Now more than ever is the most dangerous time to not know how to defend your assets.

The reason is because of the era we live in, which is the era of lawsuits. Trying to sue somebody about any little thing, which is the main reason why the court systems are backed up today. Understand that obtaining a lot of assets not only makes you independent and wealthy it also makes you a target for those who seek to exploit it. The United States has a unique problem in which it suffers from civil litigation more than any other country. Civil litigation refers to a legal dispute between two or more parties that seek money damages or specific performance rather than criminal sanctions.

When it comes to these forms of litigation, the United States struggles with a unique and costly civil justice system. Tort costs in the United States as a percentage of gross domestic product, are far higher than those of other countries. According to a 2006 study it was double the cost in Germany and more than double the cost in France or the United Kingdom. What's even crazier according to F. William Houraney, the amount that is spent on tort litigation every year is greater than what Americans spend every year on new automobiles. Suing someone for their assets in the United States is big business.

This is especially unique to Americans because of the law culture we hold, which is a litigation culture rather than an enforcement culture, giving lawyers most of the power. This is far from the case in other countries. Most European countries have adopted what they call a *"loser pay rule"*. Meaning if you sue and lose, you have to pay the other side's cost. In turn making people think a lot harder before they decide to file a suit.

Unfortunately for us blacks in America, we do not have the luxury of stopping people who wish to exploit us. We see these types of exploitation happen all the time in the real world. Two people who agree to have consensual sex, then one party gets mad and then it turns into a rape charge for money. There are lawsuits on businesses where two people get into a fight in the store, and proceed to knocking items off the shelf and slipping on them, hurting themselves. They then turn around and sue the store and win the lawsuit. These can be nightmares for individuals and small businesses alike, who are looking to defend and protect their assets, that they have worked long and hard for but can be robbed of within a short period of time through lawsuits.

It is important to remember though that there are always laws that can be used to counter these types of situations. Understanding that certain assets should be protected from being lost and such circumstances, lawmakers have passed acts under which certain types of assets are protected or can be shielded. Moving forward let's discuss these laws and other ways one can defend their assets from being attacked or garnished, from bankruptcy, divorce, or lawsuits.

Retirement Accounts

Creditors might come after your assets because you lost a lawsuit, or you have unpaid debt. This could unfortunately in return force you to file for bankruptcy. Contributions and earnings in your traditional IRA and Roth IRA have an inflation-adjusted protection cap of $1,000,000 from bankruptcy proceedings. The Bankruptcy Court has the discretion to increase this cap in the interest of justice according to Investopedia. Yet your IRA account can remain subject to federal taxes such as child support. Also, inherited IRA accounts that you may obtain from a family member isn't protected from bankruptcy unless you inherit the account from your spouse.

Other than that, the good news is getting money into a 401k and IRA is a great way to get creditors protection, says Pittsburgh Accountant and Attorney James Lange. Also, Adam Bergman of New York's IRA Financial Group said, "if you have a judgement against you and you don't file for bankruptcy, most states will still protect your IRA from the judgment". This makes IRA's and 401ks a pretty safe place to store our long-term wealth for the future without the risk of it being lost in a lawsuit.

Real Estate

Real estate is an area of your assets that most times holds the most weight. For many of us it is the biggest part of our net worth. This means it is the first asset usually threatened to be taken away in a case of a lawsuit. In today's time all it takes is one lawsuit and your house is gone. That's if you don't know how to protect your house, along with other forms of real estate you might possess.

The first basic part to protecting your real estate is

having insurance. For example, we always think of home insurance for events such as natural disasters, but it should be known that beyond covering the structure and contents of your home, homeowner's insurance has the added benefit of providing you with liability coverage for a wide array of potential claims such as your tree falls and causes damage to your neighbor's roof, your dog bites someone, someone slips and falls on your icy porch, your kid's baseball shatters your neighbor's window, your washing machine floods and destroys the neighbor's priceless alpaca rug. The point is it doesn't always have to be your house that is affected for insurance to protect you. Another key thing all our young entrepreneurs should know is that some homeowner's insurance policies cover your in-home business, even though it's very rare, you should check with your insurance company. If not most insurance companies such as Allstate, allow you to add an optional business property coverage. You may be able to purchase additional coverage to increase the protection your homeowner's insurance policy provides for business supplies.

The Insurance Information Institute states that some insurers may allow you to increase the limit up to $10,000. For example, if your homeowner's insurance limits coverage for business property to $2,000 but a fire in your home destroys $4,000 worth of inventory, you would have to pay the $2,000 difference out-of-pocket, some insurers may even force you to pay for more than that because they don't have insurance at all to cover those materials. However, if you purchased $5,000 in optional business property coverage, you'd have enough insurance to cover in full. This is key to note if we are going to push the black community towards entrepreneurship, because according to the 2012 Global Entrepreneurship Study, more than two-thirds of businesses in the United States start at home and 59% of the established business owners continue to operate from home, a number that I'm sure has more than increased in 2021 especially with COVID-19 concerns. That's why it's important your in-home business is covered too.

As far as laws are concerned the thing to note is that the amount of protection you have on your home varies widely from state-to-state. So, it is key to understand the rules and regulations you might be able to use to protect your home in your native state. Some states offer unlimited protection, others offer limited protection and a few provide no protection at all. States such as Florida and Texas are renowned for their robust homestead exemption, making it very difficult for creditors to ever get the debtors' home. This is what OJ Simpson used to exploit the Homestead Exemption Law in 1999 in Florida.

Now if you don't know, by 1995 OJ Simpson had been acquitted of double homicide by a jury of his peers. However, in 1997 the Brown and Goldman family had won a 33.5-million-dollar civil judgement against Simpson. OJ was smart however, because despite losing the civil case he had money put up in retirement accounts that for the most part were off limits. In the OJ Simpson case, the judge ruling over the presiding ruled his retirement plan could not be used as a source of proceeds to satisfy the Judgment won by the Brown and Goldman families. Also, by 1999 Simpson had made himself well acquainted with Florida's strong Homestead Protection Law as I mentioned earlier.

Under Florida law at the time, any domicile resident of Florida could take advantage of unlimited homestead exemption. Meaning OJ property could not be touched by the Brown and Goldman families either. Simpson was able to use simple federal and state laws to avoid two of his main assets from being seized. Another way of exercising asset protection on your real estate property is by putting the title to the home in the "law risk" spouse name. For wealthy businessmen or women this might help to act as a form of asset protection, especially for situations where the businessman or woman are considered to have high-risk lifestyles or businesses.

Moving their name from the title of their home for example could help to protect them against lawsuits. The effectiveness of this strategy again varies from state-to-state, so it's critical you sit down with a lawyer and discuss it thoroughly if you're considering it to be a possibility. If one spouse has a riskier occupation or lifestyle, it can be extremely strategic to place assets in the other spouse's name. Generally, the creditors of one spouse cannot reach the separate assets of the other spouse. Therefore, asset protection in the context of marriage requires a strategy whereby valuable assets are held as under the partner with least exposure to risk.

This is where a marital property agreement, prenuptial or postnuptial agreement can be beneficial if the spouse can agree that certain assets will be separate property of the spouse with less exposure to lawsuits. For example, let's say you're a very wealthy businessman and you own a general grocery store, this is a place where thousands of people shop each and every day, that in return makes it a likely place for lawsuits to be filed against the store, based on the sheer volume coming in each and every day. Say one of your employees' spills liquid on the ground and before he can go get the proper equipment to clean it an elderly lady slips and falls because of the wet spot on the floor and breaks her hip. Because of her age and injury, she spends months in the hospital where it is determined she has died from the injury sustained at your store. Angry and in need of financial support, her family sues you and wins, forcing you to pay a settlement of $2,000,000, a price you cannot afford, forcing you to sell your business to try and cover some of the settlement. Unfortunately, you are only able to sell your business for a million dollars, still leaving another million to be paid out to your creditors.

This could force you to lose your real estate property as well, throwing your family out on the streets and homeless with no stream of income to speak of, but fortunately for you, you have a marital property agreement, that states, if you the husband a business owner occurs liabilities, you and your partner can enter into an agreement that certain value for assets will be the wife's separate property, thereby shielding those assets from the husband's creditors. This will give you the option of reducing the settlement in court, because in all actuality you are broke, because the other assets that you paid for are in your wife's name, which by contract and law is off-limits. Now of course on the other hand something you should be cautious of when utilizing this strategy of real estate protection is the word divorce. Because if a divorce should happen all of the assets that you bought and put under your spouse's title name in a marital property, prenuptial, postnuptial agreement and more, would be in fact their property. Meaning you would not have any access to them.

Thus, think carefully before placing assets in your spouse's name and the impact of a postnuptial or separate property agreement. You may protect your assets from a creditor but lose them anyway in a divorce. Another form of protection you can use without much risk is titling your home using "Tenancy by the Entirety". Not all states offer "Tenancy by the Entirety" but in states that do, it offers a great form of asset protection. "Tenancy by the Entirety" is a form of ownership that as a matter of law, can only exist between a husband and wife when they opt for it.

Basically, this means that married couples own their property together. If one spouse dies, the other spouse automatically takes over the ownership of that property, as an individual. Now as it pertains to real estate with respect to asset protection planning, a

"Tenancy by the Entirety" provides a lot of protection while the tenancy is in place. Neither spouse acting alone can transfer property out of the "Tenancy by the Entirety". Rather, the consent of each spouse is required.

That feature provides built-in asset protection, if one is sued or incurs a liability of any kind, assets held in a "Tenancy by the Entirety" are exempt. They can't be accessed to satisfy a claim that exists with just one spouse. For example, a person looking to take your home in a lawsuit would be blocked from doing so, because the other spouse could block the home's sale. However, it would not help if both spouses were sued. In addition to these real estate methods, I have provided to you, there is one simpler step you can take to protect your assets. This one can be done by simply investing.

Depending on your state's homestead exemption, it might make sense for you to just simply pay an additional principal on your mortgage rather than keeping it in your bank account. For example, if you have put $50,000 into your house down payment, mortgage payment etc., but your state has $100,000 homestead exemption, it may make sense for you to invest any extra available funds into your house rather than a bank account that could be possibly seized by creditors. This way your house itself can act as a form of asset protection.

Protecting Your Money Machines

As you might have noticed throughout this book, when speaking in terms of economic, I have challenged us as a community to somewhat become entrepreneurs. By definition, an entrepreneur is a person who organizes and operates his or her own business. This is what comes to mind most times when people think about what an entrepreneur is. However, the second part of the definition is just as important. The second part says, "taking on greater than normal financial risk in order to do so". Any entrepreneur will tell you it's not the sunny days that keep you happy it's avoiding the rainy days.

Entrepreneurs are always focused on one word, and that is risk. Most entrepreneurs who own a business have two big fears 1.) Finishing in the negative as far as money goes for a particular cycle and 2.) Having your business shut down or seized. Now for the most part rule one just has to deal pretty much with your skill level as a businessman or woman. How to market and brand your business at an efficient level.

Fear number two is what keeps most entrepreneurs up at night, because it is something you do not have control over. All you can do is prepare for rule number two as if it were guaranteed to happen. If you're going to start any business in today's world, especially being that of a small business, the best way of forming it is as a limited liability company (LLC). A limited liability company is a corporate structure whereby the members of the company cannot be held personally liable for the company's debt or liabilities. When you utilize this strategy as a business owner, you're playing chess not checkers, preparing three or four moves ahead so there are no surprises.

Now these limited liability companies are essentially hybrid entities that combine the characteristics of a corporation and a partnership or sole proprietorship, similar to that of a corporation. The availability of flow through taxation to the members of the LLC is a feature of partnership. Yet, the real question when dealing or operating an LLC is, can you be found personally liable for the claims being made in a lawsuit? The answer is most of the time no, but it does not protect you from everything. If you form your LLC correctly and manage it as a separate legal entity from your personal assets, you should be protected from most liabilities arising out of the operation of the LLC business. Here are some key notes you should keep in mind about the advantages and disadvantages of starting an LLC. First there are several advantages when creating an LLC, here are some of the big ones though.

1) Pass through taxes. There is no need to file a corporate tax return. LLC owners report their shares of profit and loss on their individual tax returns, meaning you avoid double taxation saving you a lot of money.

2.) No residency requirement. Those who own an LLC need not be US citizens or permanent residents. Making it a great opportunity for our African brothers and sisters around the world to start a well-protected business on U.S. soil.

3.) Legal protection. As stated before, creating an LLC gives you limited liability for business debts and obligations.

4.) Enhances credibility. Suppliers, and Lenders may look more favorably on your business when it's an LLC, because they won't fear the legal trouble.

Now as far as the disadvantages here are a few things you should be aware of.

1.) Limited growth potential. LLC owners cannot issue shares of stock to attract investors, which limits the ways to raise capital for your business.

2.) Lack of uniformity. An LLC can be treated differently in different states.

3.) Self-employment tax. LLC earnings can be subject to this kind of taxation.

4.) Tax recognition on appreciated assets. This could happen if you convert on existing businesses to an LLC. One more way that extra taxation can occur.

Now that you know the advantages and disadvantages of an LLC, I think you will find it a very useful option to starting your small business if you are an aspiring entrepreneur. On top of that you will find it very simple and easy to get started. Here are essentially the seven basic steps to getting your LLC off the ground and running with hopefully only a little difference depending on your state.

1.) choose a legal name and reserve it if the Secretary of State in your state does that kind of thing because not all do.

2.) Draft and file your article of incorporation with your Secretary of State.

3.) Decide who will run the business whether they be chosen managers or members.

4.) Decide how many owners will be part of the LLC, because one of the advantages of an LLC is that you're allowed to have an unlimited number of owners.

5.) Apply for a business license and other certificate specific to your industry.

6.) File form SS-4 which is a form to apply for an employer identification number, or you can apply online at the Internal Revenue Services website to obtain an employer identification number known as an EIN.

7.) Last but not least, apply for any other number required by state and local government agencies. Requirements vary from one jurisdiction to another, but generally your business most likely will be required to pay unemployment, disabilities, and other payroll taxes-you will need tax ID number counts in addition to your EIN.

These are the seven basic steps to creating an LLC. If you don't want to take these steps and do it yourself, you can always go through a third-party like Legal Zoom or NoLo. These third parties will do all the work for you for a small fee, normally costing about $300. Some other side notes however to keep your business protected are drafting an operating agreement for your LLC that spells out the details of the business arrangement including members percentage, ownership, roles, rights, and responsibilities. Although this is not required by law, having such an agreement can help to protect the LLC structure if it's challenged in court by say an internal member of your organization. These written agreements will prevent you from having to default to state operating rules.

Also, note that you don't have to hire a lawyer to set up an LLC, since the steps and state requirements are usually pretty self-explanatory. Yet when dealing with the protection of your business, it is probably a good idea to have a lawyer look over the details and go over all paperwork, just to make sure your interest is protected. You will also find it helpful to document major business proceedings and lay out some formal procedures, even though most states don't require it. Be aware of your state laws on LLC's before starting one. I will say it again as I said earlier to remind you. Some states charge annual fees and taxes that can diminish economic advantages of choosing to become an LLC.

Among LLC advantages the term pass through taxation is one you should know, meaning the profits and losses are passed through the business to the individual owning the business who reports this information on their own personal tax returns. The results can mean paying less in taxes, since profits are not taxed at the business and personal level. California for instance, charges $800 LLC tax, along with a $900 to $11,760 annual fee based on a business total annual income exceeding $250,000 so be aware.

Stocks

In part 2, we discussed in great detail a strategy to gain and create long-term wealth for you and your family in the stock market. We talk about how to protect your portfolio as it pertains to just losing money from market crashes or bad stock picks, but what about lawsuits and creditors who look to take your money? In cases of a lawsuit, a judge might allow creditors to take your stock money along with everything else pertaining to your assets in order to pay a creditor. The tricky thing about protecting stock assets, is that if you try to protect stocks only after a court judgement you might be charged with fraud and attempts to essentially hide assets, putting yourself in an even worse position than before your lawsuit. However, there are ways you can protect your stock from creditors without doing it illegally.

The key is you have to do so beforehand. Before you look into any protection strategies of stocks, always work with a local Attorney, because protection strategies like all, depend on state law. A common strategy you might find helpful are non-qualified annuities. Unlike a qualified annuity, a non-qualified annuity is not part of an employer provided retirement program and may be purchased by any individual or entity. Contributions to non-qualified annuities are made with after-tax dollars and are not deductible from gross income for income tax purposes.

Now all these state laws may vary, and you might be able to protect stocks by owning them in a non-qualified variable annuity plan. You can contribute any amount to a non-qualified variable annuity and use the money to buy stocks, mutual funds and other investments. Some states protect the cash surrender value of an annuity, while others protect death benefit. Other states may offer no protection at all. Your lawyer will have to advise you on how your native state handles annuities. You can also establish an annuity in your spouse's name or simply transfer stock ownership to your spouse.

However, as we all know, the one thing about that is losing it all in the case of a divorce. Another avenue that can possibly be taken for stock protection is through Trusts, Partnerships and LLCs. Let's start with a Trust. Domestic Asset Protection Trusts otherwise known as DAPT is a good strategy to look into as it pertains to defending your stocks along with other assets. At one time, DAPTs we're only available offshore, which is why dirty or illegal money became synonymous with offshore bank accounts. However, since 1997 several states have started to allow them. As of 2021, 17 states allow

DAPTs.

These states are Alaska, Delaware, Hawaii, Michigan, Mississippi, Missouri, Nevada, New Hampshire, Ohio, Oklahoma, Rhode Island, South Dakota, Tennessee, Utah, Virginia, West Virginia, and Wyoming. The irrevocable DAPTs found in these states are administered by an independent Trustee, who can protect your stock from creditors. These states require the Trustee to be located in the state. Some states even allow you to occasionally receive income. Setting up a DAPT can be a solid strategy to protecting your stocks and other assets. *"Now more than ever with the federal government focusing on us taxpayers moving money outside the country legally and illegally, the trend will be towards using Domestic Asset Protection Trusts not offshore trusts...... If you've already got problems, setting up a DAPT isn't going to fly; the idea is to do it before you have problems"* says Peter Gordon, a trust lawyer in Wilmington, Delaware.

An alternative to a DAPT would be a family limited partnership. A Family Limited Partnership or (FLP) is a type of partnership designed to centralize family businesses or investment accounts. Family Limited Partnerships pool a family's assets together, into one single family-owned business partnership where family members own shares. You can place your stock shares, and in return receive limited partnership shares. However, Family Partnership shares have limited value to anyone other than family members, which shouldn't be a problem for the most part because most of us will be keeping the money in the family anyway.

A third option that might also present itself is protecting your stocks through your Limited Liability Company. If you're concerned about what could happen to your investment accounts in the event of a lawsuit, you may want to consider establishing an LLC on some of your assets. A brokerage account titled in the name of your LLC could help to provide some protection from creditors. Protected by your LLC, you can buy and sell stocks and bonds, just like you would in an account that is titled differently. Finally, a basic insurance might just do the trick to ease some of your minds.

Umbrella Liability Insurance is an insurance policy that goes beyond the limits of the insurers home, auto or watercraft insurance. It provides an additional layer of security to those who are at risk for being sued due to damages to other people's property or injuries caused to others in an accident. Umbrella Insurance is very helpful when the insurance owner is sued, and the dollar limit of the original policy has been exhausted. The added coverage provided by Umbrella Insurance is particularly helpful to those members of our community who own a lot of assets or very expensive assets, who are a high risk for being sued. If you lose your lawsuit but have this form of Umbrella Insurance, it pays you back for your losses and you get to keep your stock.

Military Science

Throughout this chapter we have talked about three things. Having a warrior spirit, defending your mind, and defending your money. Topics that as a matter of fact have remained pretty consistent throughout the book and should be something, if anything, you leave this book knowing. These subject matters are obviously very important in our community and with knowledge of them, it will take the black nation a long way. However, without a way of defending yourself and your community physically, the rest essentially doesn't matter.

When you look back on our history, we had brothers like Malcolm X, Martin Luther King and Medgar Evers, all leaders in our community, who did amazing things for the black man, woman, and child. Yet all these brothers along with many more of our leaders, were either killed or exiled by the powers-that-be. Looking at our history here in the Americas, we had flourishing black communities like Rosewood, Florida and Tulsa, Oklahoma, who were doing everything I wish my people would do economically. Yet these communities were simply burned down to the ground when they got too powerful. Why is this?

From our standpoint, why is it that every time one of us rises up or we as a collective build something up, they get killed or communities burned down? It's because simply put, we as a people do not take military science serious enough. Of course, there are a few of us who take it very seriously, but for the most part we as black people would rather depend on the protection from the dominant society and the system of white supremacy than ourselves, which is downright foolish when you look at our history, not only in America but around the world. From one holocaust to another, the dominant society who we have constantly put our well-being in the hands of, has turned out to be one of our biggest and fiercest adversaries. Though this as a result should come as no surprise to us.

History has tried to remind us year after year, decade after decade, century after century that we as black people have no friends. So, at the end of the day, we can't be mad at anybody but ourselves, as we keep allowing history to repeat itself with the same outcome. We are in a jungle; you have the top of the food chain and you have the bottom of the food chain. The problem is we don't know where we fit in. As far as race relations go, you and I both know that black people are at the bottom of that pole. We receive and get little to no respect.

In 2021 just like 1921 it is open season on black people. Our mother continent is being pillaged by the day. Hell, even our indigenous land here in the Americas is being pillaged right from under our noses. Our community as a whole is under constant attack and the worst part about it is we refuse to fight back. Then we have the nerve to turn around and ask the community who continues to attack us to defend us, to stop murdering us, to stop stealing from us, to stop labeling us. After 400 years that's just not intelligent on our part.

Do you ever see a zebra just stand there and let the lions attack and eat them? Do you ever see a male lion just let another male lion walk up and take his land? The answer is no, they always fight for their lives, because they know in their minds this is my only way of survival. The zebra knows he can't have a simple conversation with the lion about his pride attacking him. The male lion knows he just can't allow another male lion to just walk up and take his land, because then he will never have a land for his own.

These animals have learned from history and they know what they have to do to secure the survival of themselves and their species. They understand where they fit on the food chain. We on the other hand are confused as a whole of where we fit, therefore it divides us as a people. For example, you have those in our community who think there is no top or bottom of the food chain because we're all one. These are the "all lives matter" or "racism doesn't exist" people. These are our brothers and sisters who have been programmed mentally and physically not to fight back.

Then you have the members in our community

209

who understand there is a food chain but are submissive to *"toe the company lines"*. They know we are being treated wrong, yet they believe the only way of creating change is through politics and nonviolent protest. No matter how long it takes or how little progress is made, they will try their best to integrate their way up the food chain. Then you have the third group of our community who are not programmed by the dominant society mentally or physically. Therefore, understanding where we fit on the food chain and what strategy it would take to rise up and get to the top of the food chain.

These are members of our community who like me, have developed the independent mindset and who have taken the Malcolm X approach, by any means necessary. Malcolm X said, *"be peaceful, but courageous, obey the law, respect everyone; but if someone puts his hands on you, send him to the cemetery"*. Malcolm also said, "we are non-violent with people who are nonviolent with us .....concerning nonviolence, it is criminal to teach a man not to defend himself when he is the constant victim of brutal attacks". You see we get the oppression from the dominant society that our great ancestors like Malcolm X were promoters of violence. When in fact he was a promoter of self-defense, the same as the so-called founding fathers and governments of this country, which is why in honor of Malcolm, I'm going to give you some essential must haves in order to defend yourself and family physically, by any means necessary.

1.) Pre-Warfare (Preparation)

War is inevitable, therefore the one who is most prepared is usually the victor. There are three main keys to Pre-Warfare, Planning, Repetition and Deception. Before the war kicks off one must always have a plan on what to do and how to execute. A lack of a plan leads to mistakes and these mistakes lead to you or someone you love possibly losing their life. Therefore, in the planning stages of war three things should be known.

The first is strength and weaknesses, not only for yourself but for your enemy. We should all know when it comes to defending ourselves and our family where we are strong and where we are weak. To form a proper attack, plan catered to our strengths and defensive plan catered to our weaknesses. Knowledge of our enemies' strengths and weakness will also help us understand where to attack or where, when and who to avoid. After this has been identified, the second step is playing your role. One thing that many times causes us to lose the war is the lack of playing our role.

Everyone can't be the hero; we have too many generals trying to be soldiers and to many soldiers trying to be politicians and vice versa. It is a must that everyone knows their role and plays it accordingly, otherwise mistakes will happen, and lives will be lost. Last but not least, one must always have an exit strategy. Often times we lose wars because we simply did not regroup and re-strategize. Never get emotional in times of war and start fighting based strictly off ego, because this will cause more harm than good.

As a result, you will go from simply losing a battle to losing the entire war. Exit strategies are put into place so that one will have the opportunity to turn that loss into a lesson that can be bounced back from. Now once one has established the planning phase, the next is the repetition phase. This is simple, practice makes perfect. Your plan should be prepped out amongst you and your family on a weekly basis. This will make everyone including yourself, familiar and comfortable with the plan, in order to execute as fast and smooth as possible because you can make mistakes during practice but not during the real thing.

The last phase of preparation is arguably the most important but forgotten about and that is deception. Your plan, roles, and training etc. should not exist outside of you and your family. People should never know what you are capable of and in fact they should think you are the complete opposite of what you are. The great Sun Tzu once said "Hence, when we are able to attack, we must seem unable; when using our forces, we must appear inactive; when we are near, we must make the enemy believe we are far away; when far away, we must make him believe we are near." All warfare is based on deception, it is our goal to make our enemies believe that we never even prepared.

2.) Hand to Hand

Once the war has begun the most basic form of combat is hand to hand. A war form that all of us need weekly training on if we are going to successfully defend ourselves. Yet, before we do that a major key is first being in shape. 2020 studies done by the CDC have shown that the most obese group of people in the United States are black people with nearly 50% of our population being overweight. Family, we will never be prepared for war if most of our soldiers are too big to strap up their boots. We have to begin as a community to get on a consistent workout and eating plan in order to be ready for combat, because our hand-to-hand combat skills will only be as good as the physical shape, we are in.

Now once we do this, I would suggest we start with the basic forms of hand-to-hand combat first, like boxing. Boxing is great for building your hand-to-hand combat skills as well as getting in shape. Monthly spars would be a great exercise for building your confidence in combat situations. Next you might want to take a little kickboxing training to learn how to incorporate your feet in your combinations. Most people only use hands in combat situations, so much so that scientific studies have shown our hands have literally evolved over time for fighting.

However, what most people forget is that your

legs and feet are the most powerful body part you have. Hitting someone with the right kick or knee could put them to sleep faster than any punch could. Therefore, adding kick boxing to your repertoire would be good for your skillset. After this, there are a ton of different advanced mixed martial arts you can take, Judo, Jujitsu, Karate, Muay Thai and more. Which one you choose is up to you, as they all have their advantages. Now I understand that all these disciplines can be a bit overwhelming, but I would suggest that you take up and attempt to master at least one fight discipline. For the skill that you acquire is knowledge that you can pass on to the babies.

3.) Choppa Action

To keep it simple it is a must in 2021 for every black person to legally own firearms. However, it's not just good enough to own one, you have to be willing to actively train with it in order to become a better shooter. I would also suggest getting a license to carry in states that permit. Because I'd rather you have one and not need it, than need it and not have one. Understand that legally owning firearms does not make you scary or a criminal, it simply makes you prepared. We are living in an era where the police department has been completely infiltrated by white supremacists, and the powers that be seem unwilling to do anything about it.

As a result, this means we can't depend on the police to protect us, we must protect ourselves. With that being said I want to discuss three types of guns that all black people should own. The first is a handgun. These are guns that can be held with a single hand and are the smallest of all the firearms. For those who have a carry permit, handguns give you the ability to conceal with ease allowing you to operate in a very deceptive manner.

Now when choosing this handgun, I would encourage the family to at least get a 9-millimeter as far as caliber goes. The reason why is that 9 millimeters give you the most options as far as handgun choices, while at the same time packing a bigger punch then say a .22 or a .38 caliber handgun. As far as price goes there are good quality 9-millimeter handguns at a wide array of price points. If you are looking for one on the cheaper end, I would suggest a 9- millimeter like the Tarus G2C that you can get pretty much anywhere from between $200 to $300. If you are looking for a higher quality gun that is more durable and accurate you might want to look at something like a Glock 19 Gen 4 or 5, which is going to cost you anywhere between $600 to $800. Glock is the handgun of choice for most law enforcement agencies giving it the reputation of being very reliable in combat situations.

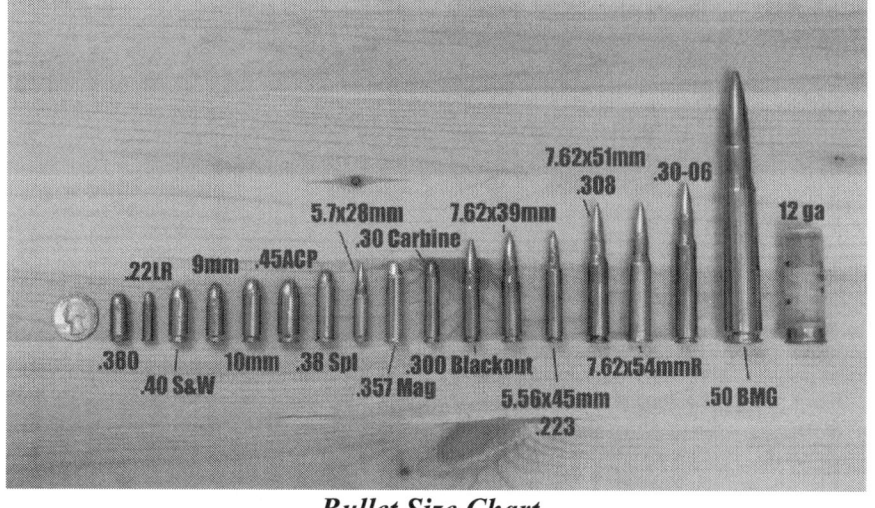

Bullet Size Chart

Now the second type of Gun that all black people should have, is a semi-automatic rifle. These guns are great for property and car defense, giving the user not only more fire power but the ability to hit a target from a longer distance, something that might come in handy when outnumbered. A rifle I would suggest everyone gets is an AR-15, preferably one that shoots .556 and .223 caliber bullets. The first reason why I suggest this gun is because it is currently the most popular rifle in the United States, meaning it is very easy to get bullets, parts, and accessories for the gun. It also means price ranges are very flexible on the gun seeing that they are very popular.

You can get a reliable but cheap AR like the Smith & Wesson M&P 15 Sport II for roughly $800. The same price you would spend on a solid handgun like a Glock. AR-15s like the M&P Sport that I just mentioned also give you an advantage, due to the 30 round magazines that they hold, giving you the ability to shoot 30 straight shots without reloading. AR-15s also have options of 50 and 100 round drums when things get really ugly, making them perfect for any situation.

Finally, the third and final gun all black people should have is a shotgun. The thought processes behind having a shotgun are simple, you need something with power. A shotgun is perfect for home defense, mainly because one blow from it usually stops any enemy in their tracks, while at the same time not over penetrating. By over penetrating I mean that the bullets from a shotgun shell will not go through a wall, hitting say a child in another room sleeping. There are several different types of shotguns, 10 Gauge, 12 Gauge, 16 Gauge, 20 Gauge, and .410 Bore.

My personal favorite is a 12 Gauge and that would be the one I suggest. However, the most important thing is not the Gauge in my opinion but the shell. Shells that are best for personal defense are double (00) or triple (000) aught buck. These shells have fewer pellets inside, but they are much larger, packing a bigger punch then 8.5, 7, 6, 4, 2 and BB shots. Other options are shooting shotgun slugs, which pack an even bigger punch, but unfortunately, over-penetrate, which is not something we want when using a shotgun. As far as prices go, similar to rifles and handguns, shotguns have a wide range of prices. However, I believe on the lower end of prices you can find some good quality shotguns, such as the

Remington 870 pump shotgun that can be purchased for $300 to $500. This is a shotgun that is still used by a lot of police departments today.

4.) Escape Plan

When it comes to having an escape plan, the name of the game is resources, and it's your access to these resources that will determine how successful your plan is. There are two types of resources one must have. The first is immediate access to capital. God forbid, but there might be a situation where as a result of war, you and your family have to leave the country, you won't have time to liquidate your assets, and this is why you need immediate access to capital. In my neighborhood we call it shoebox money, no bank or ATM required just get it and go.

Understand that in the aftermath of war, money more than anything else buys you time. Time that can be used to regroup and re-strategize, which is why I say you need access to 3 types of currencies at all times, the Dollar, Bitcoin and Gold. The dollar is important because since the end of World War II, the dollar has been the world's most important currency. It is the most commonly held reserve currency and the most widely used currency for international trade and other transactions around the world. Therefore, you should have no problem exchanging it around the world.

However, at the same time, the dollar as we know it is also losing value by the year, especially the dollars sitting in your shoebox. This is where your immediate access to gold and bitcoin come in, resources that can be used as currency but are also assets that can increase in value. Don't just let thousands of dollars stack up in your shoebox or bank. Take some of it and invest it in solid gold coins or real 24 karat gold jewelry, items that hold their value and are universally accepted everywhere. It's the same with cryptocurrency like Bitcoin, a commodity that has skyrocketed since 2013 to over $30,000. Bitcoin is also an item that can be accessed from anywhere in the world through bitcoin ATMs. So as stated before immediate access to capital is important.

The second resource you'll need in order to have a successful escape plan is human resources. It's like the old saying goes, "It's not what you know it's who you know". We must get out of the lone wolf mentality as a people and begin to grow and work together as a team. You need to have friends in all different walks of life, from the streets to the corporate world, enabling you to have people to fall back on in case of a loss. This is the reason why even some of the strongest world powers have allies, not to share in victory, but to ensure reinforcements in case of defeat.

Conclusion

As our beloved ancestor Dr. John Henrik Clarke once said, "We as black people have no friends". We have no allies or partners. We are all we have as a people. The only people who are going to defend us is us, and it all starts with our three keys to liberation and salvation as black people, knowledge of self, economics, and military science. In this section we spoke from the military science point of view, which is equally important as the other two, because what's the point of gaining an empire if you allow anybody and everybody to take it from you. From your mind to your body to your economic state of mind, knowing how to defend it will be the key to the longevity of our empires.

The art of defense is exactly what it says an art. Something that must be molded and crafted over time, but once mastered can never be taken away. You have to think like a boxer and understand in the system of white supremacy, it's nothing they want more than to see us knocked out. They will even let you build yourself up, just so they can knock you down. Fattening the pig for Slaughter. Yet, with that being said, the fact that you know this is your greatest advantage. History has presented us with enough evidence to let us to know they are looking for The Knockout Punch. Looking for any way to take our people out. That's why like Mayweather or Ali, our defense has to be sharp, because a good defense always sets up a good offense.

"The Art of War teaches us to rely not on the likelihood of the enemies not coming, but on readiness to receive him; not on the chance of his not attacking, but

rather on the fact that we have made our position inaccessible".

- Sun Tzu

Part. 4

At Last

At last, my kings and queens we have reached the end of this knowledge field journey. I hope you have learned just as much knowledge reading this book as I have writing it. When I first started writing the Voice of the Ancestors series, in my sophomore year-in college, I thought I knew it all. It was strictly my sole purpose to input the knowledge that I had learned over the years into book format and give it to you. However, as I was writing this book, I realized that I had barely scraped the iceberg of knowledge, wisdom, and information, and that it just wasn't my generation that was lost, but some of our parents and grandparents' generations as well. Generations that had been miseducated and misled to think they were nothing but slaves.

Yet as I and many other scholars who came before me have proven, we were much more than that. That's why now that you have read my book, I don't want you to think this is some new knowledge I have brought forward. The knowledge and truths have been recorded decades, even centuries before me and you were even here. Just take a look at what our ancestors left us on the walls and in the coffins of Kemet. Look at the evidence of what they left you on the Mississippi River. Take a look at the statues and artifacts they left on every continent around the world. Most of all, take a look at their lives and what they went through, from the good to the bad in order to learn from it.

Understand that the greatest gift about being so called *"woke"* is realizing how much you don't know, something that continues to be a motivating factor for me to properly educate myself. See, many of us pray for the rain but don't want to work through the thunder and lighting. The Great ancestor Frederick Douglass once said, *"I prayed for 20 years but received no answer until I prayed with my legs"*. That's the message our ancestors wanted us to receive. That your prayers will be answered when you do because the God is in you. We as a people have the ability to rise ourselves up from the ashes, but it starts right now, we can't wait any longer.

Therefore, it is important to take the knowledge you may have learned in this book and spread it to the masses of our people in order to build on that knowledge. If you see a young sister or brother who might be lost, just maybe drop a little knowledge on them. Some will accept it, others will reject it, that's for the ancestors to decide. But if you read this book, you were chosen, and that is something you have to take advantage of and be thankful for. It's time for us to put our petty differences aside and as a community get on code and work together, so that we can reach the level of power and respect we were once at.

That's why I challenge everyone who is reading this book to find the God within. Because once you do that you will understand how your talents will best benefit our people. In closing I leave you with this, a simple question. When other races look back at their history, they talk about their ancestors as if they were the best ever. They call them kings and queens even if that wasn't the case. They go out their way to make sure their generations today remember them as being great. So, my question to you my black brothers and sisters is simple. How will our descendants, a hundred years or even a thousand years from now look at us? What legacy will they see? That of lost slaves or that of kings and queens? Will they see us as Niggas or as Gods? The choice is ours.

Sources

Part. 1

- "Benjamin Banneker." BNL
- ANTL-WEISER W, 2009: The time of the Willendorf figurines and new results of Palaeolithic research in Lower Austria.
- ROGERS, J. A. Sex and Race: Negro-Caucasian Mixing in All Ages and All Lands. Vol. 1, HELGA M. ROGERS, 1967.
- Riedweg, Christoph (2005), Pythagoras: His Life, Teachings, and Influence, Ithaca, New York: Cornell University Press.
- Huffman, Carl. "Pythagoras." Stanford Encyclopedia of Philosophy, Stanford University, 17 Oct. 2018.
- Full Text of "A Monograph on Albinism in Man".
- Pliny, and Jones. Natural History, Volume VII: Books 24-27. Harvard University Press, 1956.
- Snowden, Frank M. Blacks in Antiquity Ethiopians in the Greco-Roman Experience. Harvard Univ. Pr., 1970.
- "Accessibility Navigation." Africans in Roman York?, Press Release, 26 Feb. 2010
- Ivory Bangle Lady - Roman York - Yorkshire Museum.
- Bulbeck, David, "Craniodental Affinities of Southeast Asia's "Negritos" and the Concordance with Their Genetic Affinities", November 2013.
- Demeter F, Shackelford L, Westaway K, Duringer P, Bacon A-M, Ponche J-L, et al. (2015) Early Modern Humans and Morphological Variation in Southeast Asia: Fossil Evidence from Tam Pa Ling, Laos. PLoS ONE 10(4): e0121193.
- "Lecture 4: Inside the Contact Zone: Part 1." ABC Radio National, Australian Broadcasting Corporation, 1 Nov.

2006,

- "Budj Bim, a 6000-Year-Old Aboriginal Engineering Site, Earns World Heritage Status." WEC 2019, 10 July 2019.
- Pascoe, B. (2016). Dark emu, black seeds: Agriculture or accident? Broome: Magabala.
- Galaup La Pérouse Jean-François de, et al. A Voyage Round the World in the Years 1785, 1786, 1787 and 1788. Printed for J. Johnson 1798.
- Tcherkezoff, Serge. "A Long and Unfortunate Voyage Toward the Invention of the Melanesia-Polynesia Distinction 1595–1832". Journal of Pacific History. 2003.
- Karafet, T., Mendez, F., Sudoyo, H. et al. Improved phylogenetic resolution and rapid diversification of Y-chromosome haplogroup K-M526 in Southeast Asia. Eur J Hum Genet. (2014)
- Bronwen Douglas, and Chris Ballard. Foreign Bodies: Oceania and the Science of Race 1750–1940.
- Ann Gibbons Oct. 3, 2016, et al. "'Game-Changing' Study Suggests First Polynesians Voyaged All the Way from East Asia." Science, 26 Oct. 2018.
- Lesniewski, David, "When did the ancestors of Polynesia begin to migrate to Polynesia? The mtDNA evidence" (2009). UNLV Theses, Dissertations, Professional Papers, and Capstones. 83.
- Corley, Susan J, "The British Press Greets the King of the Sandwich Islands: Kamehameha II in London, 1824" (2008)
- Douglas v. Askman, A Royal Traveler: American Press Coverage of King Kalākaua's 1881 Trip Around the World. (2017)
- Kimberly R. Norton, "Black People are Indigenous to the Americas: Research Material for Inquisitive", (2016)
- Pigafetta, Antonio, and R. A. Skelton. Magellan's Voyage a Narrative Account of the First Circumnavigation. Dover Publ.

- Wilford, J. On Crete, New Evidence of Very Ancient Mariners. (2010, February 15)
- Imhotep, D. The First Americans Were Africans: Revisited. Bloomington, IN: AuthorHouse. (2012)
- Van Sertima, I. Early America Revisited, p. 199. New Brunswick, NJ: Transaction Publishers. (1998)
- Reed, W. E. (2007, February 12). Jean-Baptiste-Point DuSable (1745-1818).
- Joseph Hodge | Social Activist | Hilbert College. (n.d.).
- Yorks Islands (U.S. National Park Service). (n.d.).
- California: What's In a Name? | UC Geography. (n.d.).
- The Life and Times of Pío Pico, Last Governor of Mexican California. (2020, August 5). KCET.
- Hudson, Charles M. Knights of Spain, Warriors of the Sun. University of Georgia Press (1997)
- Tribou, D. (2020, February 10). Elijah McCoy, African-American inventor from Michigan, changed railroad industry. Michigan Radio.
- Who Was Dr. Daniel Hale Williams? | Jackson Heart Study Graduate Training and Education Center. (n.d.).
- Massey, G. (2011). Ancient Egypt: Light of the World Vol. 1 and 2 Complete with Biography and Poems by Gerald Massey. ZuuBooks.
- Mark, J. J. (2021, January 9). Scipio Africanus the Elder. Ancient History Encyclopedia.
- Osaze, J. G. (2016). 7 Little White Lies: The Conspiracy to Destroy the Black Self-Image (1st ed.). African Genesis Institute Press.
- Deutsche Welle (n.d.). Ahmed Baba: Timbuktu's famous scholar.
- Mark, J. J. (2021, January 11). Carthage. Ancient History Encyclopedia.
- Cartwright, M. (2021, January 11). Nok Culture. Ancient History Encyclopedia.

- Nok - Art & Life in Africa - The University of Iowa Museum of Art. (n.d.).
- The maritime landscape of Kilwa Kisiwani and its region, Tanzania, 11th to 15th century AD. (2008, September 1). ScienceDirect.
- Ibn Battuta in East Africa. (n.d.). Rowan Edu.
- Cartwright, M. (2021b, January 13). Kilwa. Ancient History Encyclopedia.
- Mutapa Empire - New World Encyclopedia. (n.d.).
- Williams, C. (2020). Destruction of Black Civilization: Great Issues of a Race from 4500 B.C. to 2000 A.D.
- Ali, Ismail Mohamed (1970). Somalia Today: General Information. Ministry of Information and National Guidance, Somali Democratic Republic.
- Cassanelli, Lee V. (1982). The Shaping of Somali Society: Reconstructing the History of a Pastoral People, 1600–1900. University of Pennsylvania Press.
- Shelley, Fred M. (2013). Nation Shapes: The Story behind the World's Borders
- National Geographic Society. (2020, March 4). Great Zimbabwe.
- Editorial Team. (2019, July 31). Kingdom of the Kongo. Think Africa.
- Cartwright, M. (2021c, January 14). Kingdom of Kongo. Ancient History.
- Quiros, P. F. (n.d.). The voyages of Pedro Fernandez de Quiros, 1595-1606, Volume 1 of 2.
- Jennings, R. (2008, November 17). "Negritos" celebrated as early Taiwan settlers. U.S.
- Lothal: Sanitary drainage at the acropolis | Harappa. (n.d.).
- Morris, A.E.J. History of Urban Form: Before the Industrial Revolutions (Third ed.). New York: Routledge. (1994)
- Rashidi, R. (2012). African Star Over Asia: The Black Presence in the East. Unbranded.
- Shirley. Your Most Humble Servant. Messner, 1971.

- Griaule, Marcel. Conversations with Ogotemmêli: An Introduction to Dogon Religious Ideas. Published for the International African Institute by the Oxford University Press, 1970.
- Melanin the Secret of the Universe." Scribd.
- Amerman, Don. "The Health Benefits of Melanin." LIVESTRONG.COM, Leaf Group, 3 Oct. 2017.
- Brenner, Michaela, and Vincent J. Hearing. "The Protective Role of Melanin Against UV Damage in Human Skin." Current Neurology and Neuroscience Reports., U.S. National Library of Medicine, 2008.
- Chamary, JV. "Science Says Superman Should Be Black." Forbes, Forbes Magazine, 11 Apr. 2016.
- Taylor, Susan C. Brown Skin: Dr. Susan Taylor's Prescription for Flawless Skin, Hair, and Nails. Amistad, 2003.
- Moore. "7 Little Known Benefits of Having Melanin Rich Skin." Atlanta Black Star, Atlanta Black Star, 7 Nov. 2016.
- Sanburn, Josh. "White Deaths Exceed Births in 17 US States." Time, Time, 29 Nov. 2016.
- Tavernise, Sabrina. "Fewer Births Than Deaths Among Whites in Majority of U.S. States." The New York Times, The New York Times, 20 June 2018.
- James, George G. M. Stolen Legacy: the Egyptian Origins of Western Philosophy. Echo Point Books & Media, LLC, 2016.
- PeoplesWorld.org, Special to. "Today in History: Morocco Is the First Country to Recognize the U.S." People's World, 18 Dec. 2015.
- Moorish Civic Relation Concepts - LESSON BOOK _14." Scribd, Scribd.
- Pt. IV. Letters Official and Private, from the Beginning of His Presidency to the End of His Life: (v. 10) May, 1789-November, 1794.

- Rummel, Erika. Jiménez De Cisneros: on the Threshold of Spain's Golden Age. Arizona Center for Medieval and Renaissance Studies, 1999.
- Mackey, Albert Gallatin. The Symbolism of Freemasonry: Illustrating and Explaining Its Science and Philosophy, Its Legends, Myths and Symbols. CreateSpace, 2013.
- Schiavello, Michael. Know Thyself: Using the Symbols of Freemasonry to Improve Your Life. Lewis Masonic, 2016.
- Calcott, Wellins. A Candid Disquisition of the Principles and Practices of the Most Ancient and Honourable Society of Free and Accepted Masons: Together with Some Strictures on the Origin, Nature, and Design of That Institution ... Reprinted by W. M'Alpine, 1772.
- A Brief History of the Pythagorean Theorem." The Golden Ratio.
- Dave. "Marcus Garvey 1887-1940." AS Templates
- Delany.", "Martin R. "Martin R. Delany." The Columbia Encyclopedia, 6th Ed, Encyclopedia.com, 2018.
- "Black Star Line (1919-1923) | The Black Past: Remembered and Reclaimed." Boley, Oklahoma (1903-) | The Black Past: Remembered and Reclaimed.
- Baruch, Ruth-Marion, and Pirkle Jones. "The Black Panthers: Revolutionaries, Free Breakfast Pioneers."
- "Nation of Islam (1930–) | The Black Past: Remembered and Reclaimed." Boley, Oklahoma (1903-) | The Black Past: Remembered and Reclaimed.

Part. 2

- UGA Report: Minority Groups Driving U.S. Economy." UGA Today, 12 Dec. 2017.
- "Black Men In America.com." Black Men In Americacom.
- Chen, Liyan. "Meet The Chinese American Bank That Wants To Become Wells Fargo." Forbes, Forbes Magazine, 20 Jan. 2016.

- "DIGITAL BANKING." Personal Banking, Business Loans, and Mortgages | East West Bank.
- Williams, W. (n.d.). Black-Owned Banks by State. Investopedia.
- Anderson, Claud. PowerNomics: the National Plan to Empower Black America. PowerNomics Corp. of America, 2001.
- "Directory of Black Owned Banks & Credit Unions In The USA - 01/20/2016.
- "U.S. Map of Black-Owned Banks." BLACKOUT Coalition.
- "Dr. Martin Luther King Jr: 'I Fear I Am Integrating My People into a Burning House'." New York Amsterdam News: The New Black View.
- Finley, Taryn. "Black Banks Are In Decline. This Group Wants To Show How Much They Matter." The Huffington Post, TheHuffingtonPost.com, 9 Feb. 2017.
- "Justice Department Sues KleinBank for Redlining Minority Neighborhoods in Minnesota." The United States Department of Justice.
- "Manhattan U.S. Attorney Settles Lending Discrimination Suit Against JPMorgan Chase For $53 Million." The United States Department of Justice, 23 Jan. 2017.
- "Federal DepositInsurance Corporation." FDIC: BankFind Home.
- "Home." National Credit Union Administration.
- Staff, Marketplace. "The Bank Black Movement Gains Traction." Marketplace, Marketplace.
- Badger, Emily. "Whites Have Huge Wealth Edge Over Blacks (but Don't Know It)." The New York Times, The New York Times, 18 Sept. 2017.
- Only 49% of Americans have any money in stocks at all. "Who's Getting Rich off the Stock Market?" CNNMoney, Cable News Network.

- Chamaria, Neha. "5 Top Dividend Kings to Buy and Hold Forever." The Motley Fool, The Motley Fool, 22 June 2018.
- "Dow Jones - 100 Year Historical Chart." MacroTrends.
- Hulbert, Mark. "The Road Back From the '29 Crash Wasn't So Long, After All." The New York Times, The New York Times, 25 Apr. 2009.
- Roth, Allan. "Compound Interest - The Most Powerful Force in the Universe?" CBS News, CBS Interactive, 7 June 2011.
- Malkiel, Burton Gordon. A Random Walk down Wall Street: the Time-Tested Strategy for Successful Investing. W.W. Norton & Company, 2019.
- Frankel, Matthew, and CFP. "How Many Stocks Does Warren Buffett Own?" The Motley Fool, The Motley Fool, 21 May 2016.
- Long, John Vincent. "Tracking George Soros's Portfolio - Q2 2018 Update." Seeking Alpha, Seeking Alpha, 2 Sept. 2018.
- Long, John Vincent. "Tracking Carl Icahn's Portfolio - Q1 2018 Update." Seeking Alpha, Seeking Alpha, 21 May 2018.
- Long, John Vincent. "Tracking David Tepper's Appaloosa Management Portfolio - Q2 2018 Update." Seeking Alpha, Seeking Alpha, 3 Sept. 2018.
- Rapacon, Stacy. "Great Mutual Funds for Young Investors." Www.kiplinger.com, Kiplingers Personal Finance, 7 Mar. 2014.
- Rich, Bryan. "Silicon Valley Has Been The Best Place To Get Rich Over The Past Decade." Forbes, Forbes Magazine, 26 Oct. 2017.
- "Invest, Save, and Learn with the Stash Investment App." Stash,
- Staff, Investopedia. "Put Option." Investopedia, Investopedia, 4 Aug. 2018.

- Jagerson, John A. "Short Selling." Investopedia, Investopedia, 5 Nov. 2018.
- "Compare Savings Account Rates." Deposit Accounts.
- "Average Stock Market Return: Where Does 7% Come From?" The Simple Dollar, 28 Mar. 2016.
- Vardi, Nathan. "Inside The Obama Stock Market's 235% Return." Forbes, Forbes Magazine, 20 Jan. 2017.
- "Does a Dollar Spent in the Black Community Really Stay There for Only Six Hours?" Truth Be Told, 18 Sept. 2018.
- Liu, Roseann. "Dismantling the Barrier between Asians and African-Americans | Commentary." , The Philadelphia Inquirer, Daily News and Philly.com, 8 June 2018.
- "Chinese Investment in Jamaica and Region Growing." The Caribbean Council, 15 Aug. 2016.
- "Montgomery Bus Boycott." Birmingham Campaign | The Martin Luther King, Jr., Research and Education Institute, 5 Dec. 1955.
- Boley, Oklahoma (1903-) | The Black Past: Remembered and Reclaimed, blackpast.org/aah/montgomery-bus-boycott-1955-56.
- Rumble, Taylor-Dior. "Claudette Colvin: The 15-Year-Old Who Came before Rosa Parks." BBC News, BBC, 10 Mar. 2018.
- "The Largest Marketplace for Black Owned Businesses." How We Buy Black.
- Marcus Garvey - Impact | Buy Black Movement.
- SB Nation NFL. "The Real Reasons Why NFL Players Are Protesting and How Their Message Gets Lost in Politics." SBNation.com, SBNation.com, 21 Oct. 2018.
- Golden State Warriors Revenue 2001-2017 | Statistic." Statista
- "Dallas Cowboys 2017 Salary Cap." Spotrac.com
- Goodman, H. A. "Colin Kaepernick Should Be Praised, Not Condemned." The Huffington Post.

- NFL. "Finalized 2017 Pro Bowl Rosters." NFL.com History, National Football League, 26 Jan. 2017.
- Bowen, Fred. "In Its Early Years, NBA Blocked Black Players." The Washington Post, WP Company, 15 Feb. 2017.
- "NBA All-Star 2018 | Roster."
- "NFL Pass Interception % Career Leaders." Pro-Football-Reference.com.
- "2017 Dallas Cowboys 53-Man Roster."
- "ESPN Football Recruiting - 300 Player Rankings." ESPN, ESPN Internet Ventures.
- Zenitz, Matt. "Projecting Alabama's 2017 Depth Chart." AL.com, AL.com, 18 Jan. 2017.
- Kercheval, Ben. "Swinney Misses Mark with Well-Intentioned Comments on Kaepernick Protest." CBSSports.com, CBS Sports, 15 Sept. 2016.
- Kenyon, David. "Clemson vs. Alabama: Position-by-Position National Championship Breakdown." Bleacher Report, Bleacher Report, 28 Sept. 2017.
- "How Diverse Is The University of Alabama?" College Factual, 27 Sept. 2018.
- "Undergraduate Ethnic Diversity at Clemson University." College Factual, 27 Sept. 2018.
- "Dabo Swinney: It's Easy to Say We Have a Race Problem, But We Have a Sin Problem." CNS News, 19 Sept. 2016.
- "Cost of Attendance | Financial Aid." The University of Alabama.
- Estimated Cost of Attendance." Criminal Justice (B.S./B.A.) | Degree Programs | Clemson University, South Carolina.
- Heim, Mark. "Gross Revenue for All SEC Football Programs for 2016-17 Fiscal Year." AL.com, AL.com, 16 May 2018.
- Gaines, Cork. "Alabama Had a Huge Advantage over Clemson off the Field, but It Will Now Start

Disappearing."
- "ESPN Basketball Recruiting - Player Rankings." ESPN, ESPN Internet Ventures.
- Wiggins, Brandon. "The 25 Schools That Make the Most Money in College Basketball." Business Insider, Business Insider, 31 Mar. 2018.
- "Historically Black Colleges and Universities in a Time of Economic Crisis." On Freedom of Expression and Campus Speech Codes | AAUP.
- Anderson, Monica. "Enrollment at HBCUs: A Closer Look." Pew Research Center, Pew Research Center, 28 Feb. 2017.
- Anderson, Nick. "Howard University's Credit Rating Cut for Third Time in Three Years." The Washington Post, WP Company, 5 June 2015.
- "What Will a Trump Presidency Mean for America's HBCUs?" NBCNews.com, NBCUniversal News Group.
- Rogin, Josh. "How China Got a U.S. Senator to Do Its Political Bidding." The Washington Post, WP Company, 17 Dec. 2017.
- California State University, Northridge. Television Statistics.
- "Unemployment for Young Black Grads Is Still Worse than It Was for Young White Grads in the Aftermath of the Recession." Economic Policy Institute.
- "School-to-Prison Pipeline." American Civil Liberties Union, Aclu.
- Nutrition & the Epigenome, learn.genetics.utah.edu
- Frye, Devon. "Childhood Ritalin Use May Have Long-Term Effects on the Brain." ADDitude, ADDitude, 8 Sept. 2017.
- Carpenter, Deborah, et al. "What Are the Symptoms of ADHD?" ADDitude, ADDitude, 16 Mar. 2018.
- Dr. Umar Johnson. Psycho Academic Holocaust: The

special education ADHD war against black boys.

<u>Part. 3</u>

- Nubian Archers | The Oriental Institute of the University of Chicago. (n.d.).
- Gabriel, R. A. (2002). The Great Armies of Antiquity: (Illustrated ed.). Praeger..
- Frederick Edwyn Forbes. Dahomey and the Dahomans, Being the Journals of Two Missions to the King of Dahomey, and Residence at His Capital, in the Year 1849 and 1850, Volume 1. Longman, Brown, Green,and Longmans.
- Hoh, A. (2020, March 31). Emperor Menelik II of Ethiopia and the Battle of Adwa: A Pictorial History | 4 Corners of the World: International Collections and Studies at the Library of Congress.
- Women in world history : a biographical encyclopedia. Commire, Anne., Klezmer, Deborah. Waterford, CT: Yorkin Publications. 1999–2002.
- 8 war heroes you didn't learn about in school. (2016, April 21). NITV.
- Osaze, J. G. (2016b). 7 Little White Lies: The Conspiracy to Destroy the Black Self-Image (1st ed.). African Genesis Institute Press.
- Rogers, J. A. (1980). 100 Amazing Facts About the Negro with Complete Proof: A Short Cut to The World History of The Negro (illustrated edition). Wesleyan University Press.
- Rashidi, R. (2021b). African Star Over Asia: The Black Presence in the East. Unbranded.
- Anatomy of the Brain." Brain Anatomy, Anatomy of the Human Brain.
- "Freud's Model of the Human Mind." Journal Psyche.
- Marcus, Gary. "Opinion | Face It, Your Brain Is a Computer." The New York Times, The New York Times,

21 Dec. 2017.

- "The Conscious, Subconscious, And Unconscious Mind –
  How Does It All Work?" The Mind Unleashed, 6 Nov.
  2014.
- "The Final Call." Willie Lynch Letter: The Making of a
  Slave.
- March 2002, From Early Child Development.
- Edie, et al. "Brain Development and Early Learning:
  Research on Brain Development. Quality Matters. Volume
  1, Winter 2007." Journal of Research in Education, Eastern
  Educational Research Association. George Watson,
  Marshall University, One John Marshall Drive, College of
  Education and Professional Development, Huntington, WV
  25755.
- "Harvard Researcher Says Children Learn Racism Quickly
  - The Boston Globe." BostonGlobe.com, The Boston
  Globe, 10 June 2012.
- "Kenneth and Mamie Clark Doll." National Parks Service,
  U.S. Department of the Interior.
- "Federal Role in Education." Home, US Department of
  Education (ED), 25 May 2017.
- Kennedy, Robert. "What's the Difference Between Private
  Schools and Independent Schools?" Thoughtco., Dotdash.
- Scott-Clayton, Judith, and Jing Li. "Black-White Disparity
  in Student Loan Debt More than Triples after Graduation."
  Brookings, The Brookings Institution, 29 Mar. 2017.
- Mulhere, Kaitlin. "Black Grads Struggle to Repay Student
  Loans, New Data Show | Money." Time, Time, 17 Oct.
  2017.
- "LIMRA: Black Americans Are More Likely to Buy Life
  Insurance Than the General Population.
- "New York Life's African-American Market Agents Have
  Achieved a Milestone of $50 Billion of Life Insurance in
  Force." Insure Invest Retire: New York Life Insurance

Company.
- "Social Security Benefits Are Modest." Center on Budget and Policy Priorities, 11 Oct. 2017.
- "Whole Life Insurance Coverage, Who Needs It?" The Simple Dollar, 16 Nov. 2018.
- "Do You Have Enough Life Insurance?" U.S. News & World Report, U.S. News & World Report.
- "Greater Justice, Lower Cost: How a 'Loser Pays' Rule Would Improve the American Legal System." Manhattan Institute, 21 Nov. 2016.
- JAMES R. MAXEINER, Cost and Fee Allocation in Civil Procedure Vol. 58, 2010.
- Carpenter, J. William. "Is My IRA Protected in a Bankruptcy?" Investopedia, Investopedia, 19 Aug. 2015.
- Clements, Jonathan. "How to Protect Your Assets from Lawsuits." MarketWatch, MarketWatch, 30 June 2014.
- Vallet, Mark. "Home Liability Insurance: What Does It Cover?" Insure.com.
- Campbell, Anita. "69 Percent of U.S. Entrepreneurs Start Their Businesses at Home." Small Business Trends, 2 July 2013.
- Novack, Janet. "Protection Time." Forbes, Forbes Magazine, 6 June 2013.
- "Archives for May 2018." The Beliveau Law Group - Attorneys at Law.
- "Tenancy by the Entirety." LawShelf Educational Media,
- Conway, Trey. "Extra Payment Mortgage Calculator." Home Mortgage Interest Deduction Calculator.
- "What Is an LLC (Limited Liability Company)?" Why & How To Incorporate in Delaware or Form DE LLC.
- "How to Start an LLC in 7 Steps." Legalzoom.com, 21 June 2017.
- Obesity is a Common, Serious, and Costly Disease. (2020, June 29). Centers for Disease Control and Prevention.
- Siripurapu, A. (2020, September 28). The Dollar: The

Voice of the Ancestors III

World's Currency. Council on Foreign Relations.

Voice of the Ancestors III

Voice of the Ancestors III

Voice of the Ancestors III

Voice of the Ancestors III

Voice of the Ancestors III

Voice of the Ancestors III

Made in the USA
Columbia, SC
24 July 2024